Contents

AF185286

Reference

Metals

1 **Use the table of chemical elements on page 49 to fill in the names of the metals.**

A metal is an element such as _____ [1] (**Fe**) and _____ [2] (**Cu**). Most metals are hard, solid, opaque and shiny when cut. They are also usually good conductors of heat and electricity. But not all metals from _____ [3] (**Al**) to _____ [4] (**Zn**) have these properties. For example, _____ [5] (**Hg**) is liquid at room temperature, while both _____ [6] (**Pb**) and _____ [7] (**Na**) are soft. We divide metals into two main groups, noble metals and base metals. The three most common noble – or 'precious' – metals are _____ [8] (**Au**), _____ [9] (**Pt**) and _____ [10] (**Ag**). These metals are used to make expensive watches, ornaments, jewellery and even artefacts like cutlery and bathroom fittings. Base metals, on the other hand, are metals like aluminium (AE: aluminum), iron, and zinc that are used to make everyday equipment. In industrial applications and engineering, we divide base metals into two further groups, namely light metals like _____ [11] (**Sn**), and heavy metals such as _____ [12] (**W**).

2 **Join a sentence part from 1–8 to one from a)–h) to make true statements about metals.**

1   Most metals are solid, but
2   We use noble metals like
3   Iron, lead and mercury are
4   Metals like iron are hard, but
5   In engineering, we divide base metals
6   Metals, particularly copper, make
7   If you cut a piece of metal in two, the ends
8   We use base metals to make articles

a)   three examples of heavy metals.
b)   gold to make expensive jewellery.
c)   that we need in our everyday lives.
d)   good conductors of heat and electricity.
e)   into heavy metals and light metals.
f)   of the pieces are usually shiny.
g)   lead and sodium are soft.
h)   mercury, for example, is a liquid.

1 _____   2 _____   3 _____   4 _____   5 _____   6 _____   7 _____   8 _____

3 **Find the captions to the photos. Then find the metals these things are made of.**

bridge • can • wheel rim • cup • pipes • watch •
watering can • thermometer • aluminium •
copper • gold • iron • mercury • silver • tin • zinc

_____   _____   _____   _____

_____   _____   _____   _____

4 Label the drawing of a furnace using words and expressions from the text below.

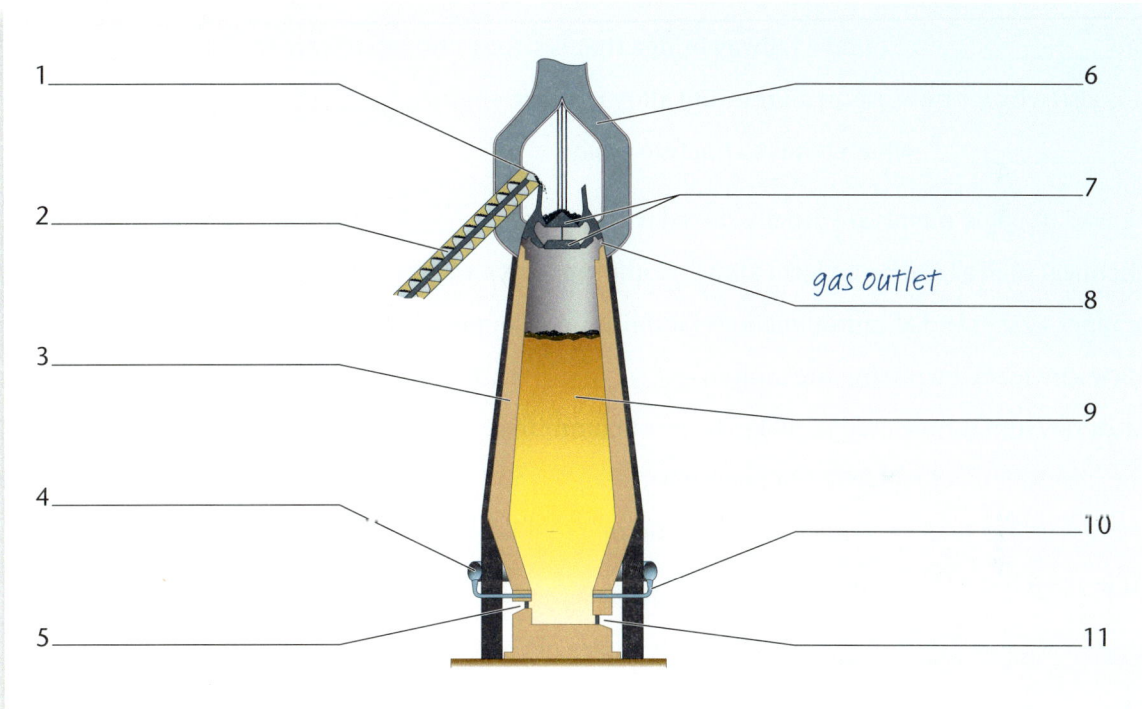

gas outlet

The inside of the furnace has a refractory lining of brick to stop heat escaping. At the top of the tower there are charging bells. They stop the ore or 'charge' from the conveyor system from falling into the furnace before it is needed. There is an exhaust gas outlet at the very top of the furnace that allows gases to escape into the atmosphere. At the bottom of the tower, preheated air from the bustle pipe is forced or 'blasted' into the furnace through pipes called tuyeres (pronounced 'two ears') to heat the mixture of coke, limestone and iron ore.

The coke burns and raises the temperature in the furnace from about 200 °C at the top, to up to 2000 °C at the bottom. The limestone works like a cleaner. It absorbs impurities in the iron ore to form a waste product called 'slag'. This floats to the top of the molten iron where it can be removed through the slag hole. As the furnace fills, the molten iron is removed or 'tapped off' through a second opening called the taphole. Most of the molten iron is taken straight from the furnace to a steel mill for further processing. However, some is poured into moulds called 'pigs'. There it cools to make pig iron, which is used to make cast-iron products.

Alloys

T 2 **1** **Work with a partner. Complete the text with words from the box. Then listen to the CD to check your answers and fill in any gaps.**

base metals • brass • brittle • carbon •
carbon steel • cast iron • copper •
cylinder blocks • impurities • iron •
pure metals • sheet steel • substances •
train • tubing • wire

What are 'alloys'?

1 In their raw state, _____ [1] like iron,

aluminium and _____ [2] are often of low quality

because of _____ [3]. Pig iron, for example, contains silica, phosphorus and sulphur that

make it _____ [4] and lower its load-bearing capacity. That is why we need huge amounts

5 of _____ [5] to build a railway bridge that is strong enough to carry a _____ [6].

It is also why we now use an aluminium alloy to make engine _____ [7] instead of

_____ [8], which tends to fracture easily.

Nowadays, pure metals are usually mixed with other _____ [9] or with a non-metal

chemical such as carbon to form alloys. Common alloys are steel (iron + carbon), _____ [10]

10 (copper + zinc) and aluminium alloys (aluminium + copper, aluminium + magnesium). These

alloys are made by mixing the molten _____ [11] and then cooling them until they solidify.

Most raw iron is now used to make the most common alloy, _____ [12], by burning off

the impurities and replacing them with between 0.5 and 1.5 per cent _____ [13]. This

process makes steel very much stronger and more malleable than iron. These properties enable

15 us to stretch steel to produce _____ [14], to cut it into strips and roll it to produce

_____ [15] and to press rolled _____ [16] to produce car bodies, for example.

2 **Write the captions beneath the photos. Then use line numbers to link the photos to the text.**

brass • cast aluminium alloy • tubular steel •
iron • pressed sheet steel • steel wire rope

_____ I. _____   _____ I. _____   _____ I. _____

_____ I. _____   _____ I. _____   _____ I. _____

3 Read the description of a basic oxygen furnace and use the drawing to put in the missing paragraph headings 1–8.

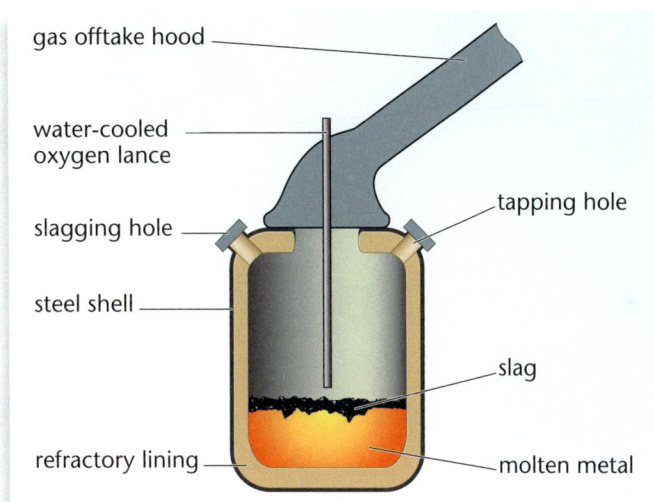

gas offtake hood

water-cooled oxygen lance

slagging hole

steel shell

refractory lining

tapping hole

slag

molten metal

1 _____

This water-cooled component supplies super-heated oxygen to the furnace.

2 _____

The next component stops toxic emissions escaping into the atmosphere. It also reduces heat loss.

3 _____

This opening is used to remove the molten steel from the furnace. This is done by tilting the steel shell to the right. During the manufacturing process, it is closed to avoid heat loss.

4 _____

These impurities float on top of the molten steel.

5 _____

This is the steel. It is "tapped off" through the tapping hole when it is the correct consistency.

6 _____

These special bricks and cement insulate the furnace against heat loss so that less energy is needed to keep it operating.

7 _____

This bottle-shaped container is the main body of the furnace.

8 _slagging hole_

This opening operates like the tapping hole. It is kept closed during the steel-making process to prevent heat loss.

Measurement

We measure the length of a steel bar or the depth of an engine cylinder by comparing these dimensions to a known quantity or 'standard', the scale on a ruler, for example. However, a ruler is often not accurate enough for many purposes. A much more accurate measuring instrument for smaller workpieces is a micrometre or vernier callipers*.

1 Look at the photos carefully and label them with a word or expression from the list.

> analogue vernier callipers • depth micrometre •
> height gauge • digital callipers • inside micrometre •
> outside micrometre • ruler • dial callipers

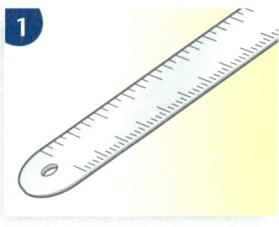 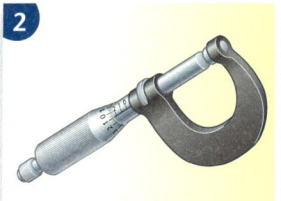 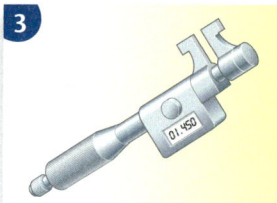 

_____ _____ _____ _____

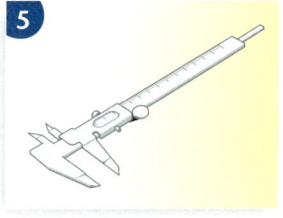 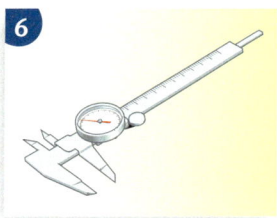 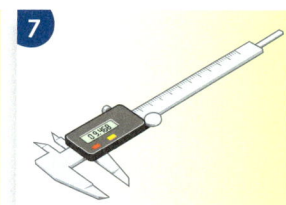 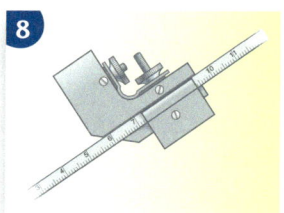

_____ _____ _____ _____

2 Complete the description with words/expressions from the illustration.

Analogue vernier callipers have two sets of _____ [1] at one end and a retractable _____ [2] at the other. The smaller jaws are for measuring _____ [3], such as the interior diameter of a pipe, and we use the larger jaws for measuring _____ [4], such as the thickness of sheet steel. The stem is for measuring the _____ [5] of a hole, for example. Vernier callipers have _____ [6], the _____ [7] with larger units and the

_____ [8] with smaller ones. Once the jaws are applied to the workpiece, a _____ [9] holds them firmly in place.

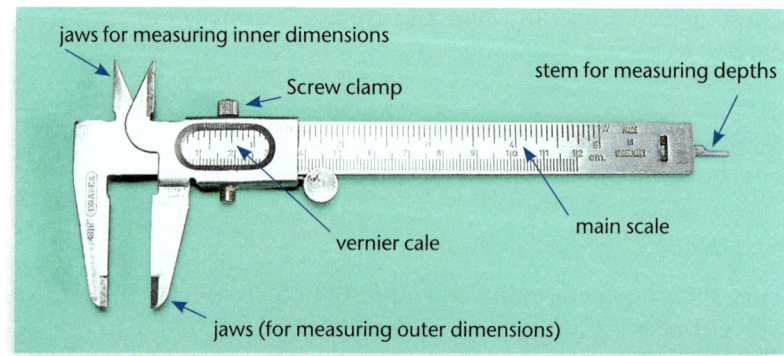

jaws for measuring inner dimensions
Screw clamp
stem for measuring depths
main scale
vernier cale
jaws (for measuring outer dimensions)

* (AE = calipers)

3 These six drawings show you the most common causes of inaccurate measurement.
Link the drawings 1–6 with the captions A–F.

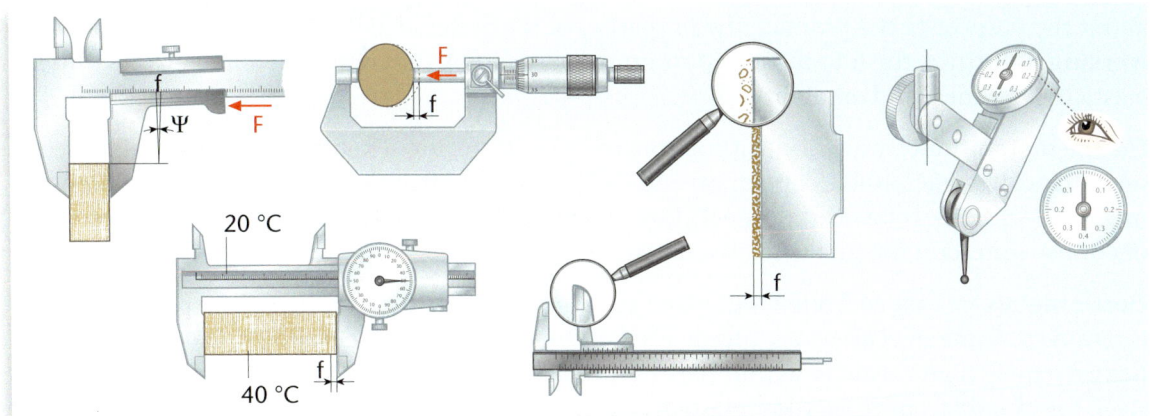

A   faulty positioning of instrument
B   change of shape caused by pressure on workpiece
C   dirt on workpiece and/or measuring surfaces

D   incorrect reading of scales
E   temperature difference
F   wear of measuring surfaces

1. _____,   2. _____,   3. _____,   4. _____,   5. _____,   6. _____

4 Measuring with a depth micrometre: Put the parts of the text into the correct order. Then
match the illustrationsto the correct parts of the text.

A _____   The piston must be at TDC (top dead centre) and the cylinder liner must be firmly
seated into the crankcase to obtain the correct measurements.

B _____   The space between the cylinder head and the top of the piston is called the squish
band. This is how to measure the squish band with a depth micrometre.

C _____   Position the piston at top dead centre. An easy way is to turn the engine upside down
and press it firmly down onto a table top while you rotate the crankshaft.

D _____   Measure the distance from the top of the cylinder to the top of the piston with a depth
micrometre as shown. Be careful that the micrometre does not push the piston off
TDC. This example measures .062".

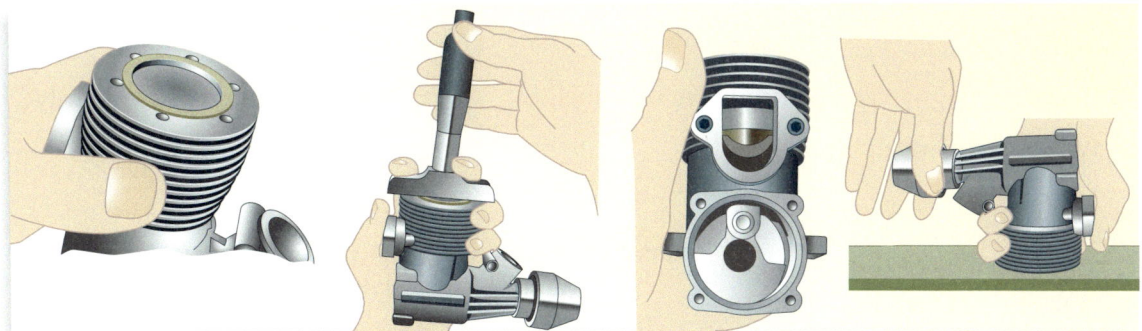

a ____   b ____   c ____   d ____

T 3   Now listen to the CD and check your results.

The properties of metals and alloys

In manufacturing, it is essential to choose the right material for the job. This means thinking about the purpose of the product, the properties of the material and, of course, its cost. In metal-working industries, the four most important properties of metals and their alloys are ductility, elasticity, hardness and durability.

Ductile metals stretch and form without breaking or fracturing. They also keep or 'retain' their new shape. Base metals like copper, tin and zinc all have high ductility when heated, as do noble metals like gold. Soft low-carbon steel alloys are quite ductile, but harder high-carbon steels and, of course, iron soon fracture when stretched.

Elastic metals are easy to stretch, but when cold they go back to their original shape when stress is removed. Some steel alloys are highly elastic. One high-carbon steel alloy called 'spring steel' has extremely high elasticity within narrow limits. Other hard steels – tool steel and stainless steel, for example – have very low elasticity or none at all.

Hard metals like cast iron and steel alloys can withstand friction without wearing. Their hardness makes them ideal for making the moving parts of machines and, in the case of steel, the cutting edges of tools. Steel alloys with a high carbon content of between 0.65% and 1.50% are harder than those with less carbon.

Durable metals do not corrode easily in air and moist conditions. Chromium (Cr) and platinum have high durability but they are expensive and in short supply. Gold, silver and some aluminium alloys are also very durable. Cast iron and low-carbon steels are not corrosion-resistant. They have to be painted or galvanized to protect them. However, some fine steels such as stainless steel and tungsten steel, often used for sawblades, are very durable.

1 Correct these six statements by replacing the highlighted words.

1 Ductile _____ metals return to their final _____ shape when stress is removed.

2 Hard metals like iron can withstand cold _____ without breaking _____.

3 The elasticity _____ of aluminium _____ alloys makes them suitable for the moving parts of machines.

4 Steel alloys with a high carbon content are more elastic _____ than those with less iron _____.

5 Copper _____ and platinum are very ductile _____, but they are also very expensive.

6 We have to paint aluminium _____ to make it resistant to wear _____.

2 Label the photos. Say what they are made of and what their most important property is.

camshaft • cans • chisel • guttering • sawblade • springs • wheel rim • wrench •
copper • high-carbon steel (2×) • low-carbon steel • spring steel • tool steel • tin • tungsten steel
ductility • durability • elasticity • hardness

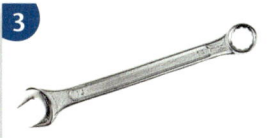

_____   _____   _____   _____

_____   _____   _____   _____

T 4 **3** First, try to complete the text with words and expressions from the list below. Then listen to the CD to check your answers and fill in any gaps.

> a) bridge • b) brittle • c) cast iron • d) engineers •
> e) elastic • f) engineering wonder • g) fracturing •
> h) high spans • i) iron bridge • j) low temperatures •
> k) railway workers • l) structure • m) supports •
> n) swayed • o) tonnes of iron • p) train •
> q) wind-stress • r) windy days

The Tay Bridge disaster

On 28 December 1879 a _____ [1] left Dundee on the Firth of Tay in eastern Scotland for Edinburgh in a bad storm. The train ran on to the new _____ [2] across the River Tay just south of Dundee, but it never reached the other end. Although the Tay Bridge was called 'an _____'[3], its 13 high spans fell down in the storm with the loss of 75 lives. What went wrong? According to the official enquiry into the cause of the disaster, _____ [4] on the 13 _____ [5] put so much strain on the 75-metre-tall iron _____ [6] that one or more of them fractured. The reason for this _____ [7] was probably that the _____ [8] used in the supports became so _____ [9] in cold weather that it was not _____ [10] enough to withstand high winds. This agreed with the opinion of passengers and _____ [11]. They said that they felt nervous on the bridge on _____ [12]. Trains sometimes rocked from side to side or '_____'[13] so much that objects fell off tables. Seamen also reported seeing the _____ [14] moving in the wind as they sailed beneath it. Yet the enquiry heard from _____ [15] that they had not thought about the effect of variable wind-stress and _____ [16] at all. They simply guessed that a massive _____ [17] made of thousands of _____ [18] could withstand anything.

Hand tools

1 Label the photos of these general tools with the words or expressions from below.

socket spanner • open-end spanner • Phillips screwdriver • pliers • flat-blade screwdriver • adjustable spanner • ring spanner • bench vice* • Allen key • hand drill

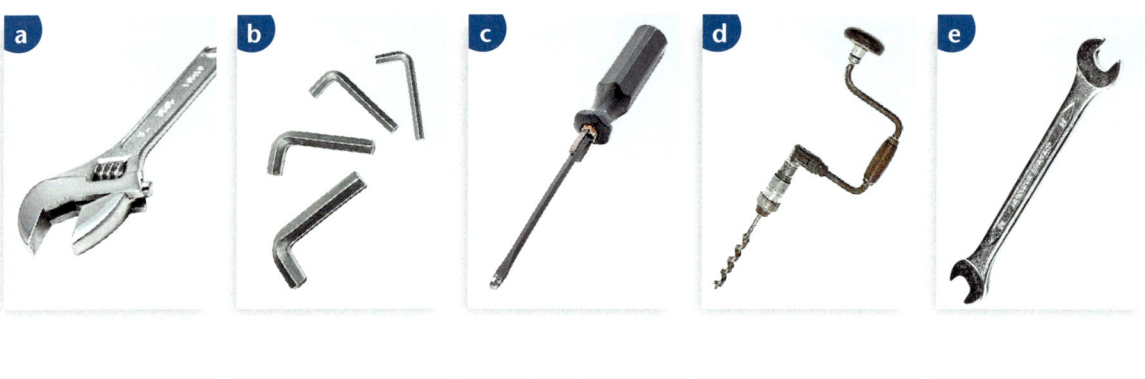

a _____

b _____

c _____

d _____

e _____

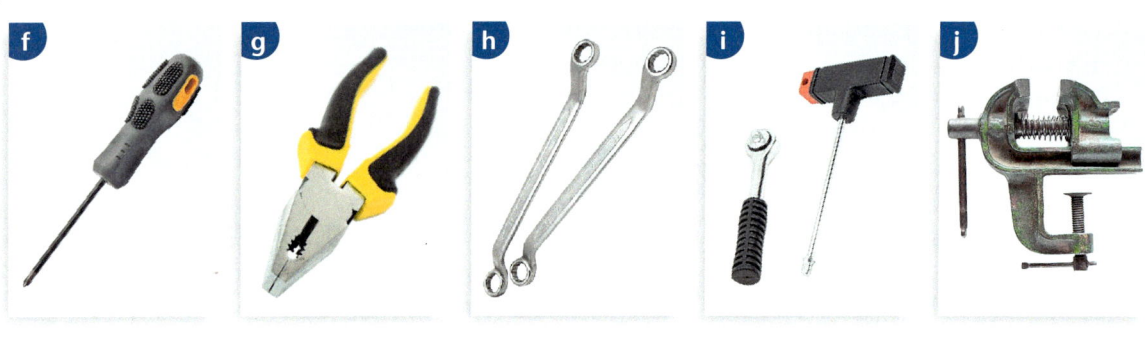

f _____

g _____

h _____

i _____

j _____

2 Which tools from above are being described here?

We use this tool to …

1	… hold the whole of the head of a nut or bolt securely while turning it.	[ ]
2	… hold a workpiece so as to free both hands to work on it.	[ ]
3	… turn screws or bolts with a cross-cut head.	[ ]
4	… turn nuts or bolts in either direction with the help of a ratchet.	[ ]
5	… drive in or remove a screw with a straight-cut head.	[ ]
6	… turn nuts or bolts of various head sizes with the same tool.	[ ]
7	… drill a hole in a block of wood.	[ ]
8	… turn nuts and bolts in very limited spaces or from only one side.	[ ]
9	… hold or 'grip' smaller workpieces with one hand while working on them.	[ ]
10	… turn screws or bolts with a hexagonal countersunk head.	[ ]

* AE: vise

3 Complete the sentences with the correct metalworking tool.

round file **tongs** **sheet metal cutters** **anvil** **half-round file**

wire cutters **ball-peen hammer** **hacksaw** **bolt cutters** **flat file**

1 Can you hand me a _____, please? I want to smooth the inside of a hole.

2 I can't remove this wheel with a wrench. I need some _____, I'm afraid.

3 Your first job is to smooth the edges of this steel bar with a _____.

4 You can't cut copper pipes with _____. You need a _____.

5 We watched a blacksmith using _____ to lift some hot iron.

6 A _____ file is useful because it's convex on one side and flat on the other.

7 Where are the _____? I need them to cut some electric cable.

8 Blacksmiths use a _____ and _____ to shape hot metal.

4 Complete the table with the names of tools from exercises 1–3. Which tool appears twice?

Cutting / drilling	Turning screws	Turning nuts/bolts	Smoothing/shaping	Holding/supporting
hand drill				

The... appears twice.

T5 5 Link the sounds to the tools.

Sound 1   **a)** hacksaw cutting copper pipe
Sound 2   **b)** coarse file smoothing steel bar
Sound 3   **c)** blacksmith hammering hot iron
Sound 4   **d)** sheet metal cutters cutting sheet steel
Sound 5   **e)** spanner loosening tight nut
Sound 6   **f)** workpiece being put in vice

1 ____   2 ____   3 ____   4 ____   5 ____   6 ____

13

Manual power tools

1 Read the clues and label the photos with an expression from the list.

cut-off saw • grinder • power buffer • power drill • power hacksaw • power screwdriver • power wrench • welding torch

Clues:

1 … is useless without the correct bit for wood or metal.
2 … is used for smoothing the rough edges of metal.
3 … has a diamond cutting wheel to cut very hard materials such as high-carbon steel.
4 … has different blades for cutting wood or metal.
5 … takes the work out of polishing a car, for example.
6 … is used to join the parts of bike frames, for example.
7 … and the one next to it develop very high torque or 'twist' to turn screws, nuts and bolts.
8 … melts solder and joins metal parts together.

1 _____   2 _____   3 _____   4 _____

5 _____   6 _____   7 _____   8 _____

2 Fill in the table below.

~~cutting hard metals, e.g. steel~~ • cutting softer metals, e.g. copper • drilling holes in metal, wood, masonry • joining metals by means of welding • polishing shiny surfaces • smoothing rough metal edges • turning nuts/bolts • turning screws

	English	German	Purpose
1	cut-off saw	Trennkreissäge	cutting hard metals, e.g. steel
2	grinder		
3	power buffer		
4	power drill		
5	power hacksaw		
6	power screwdriver		
7	power wrench		
8	welding torch		

T6 **3** **Listen to the CD and label the parts of a power screwdriver.**

battery (in handle) • chuck • chuck lock • cover • electric motor • gear train • handle • screwdriver bit • switch

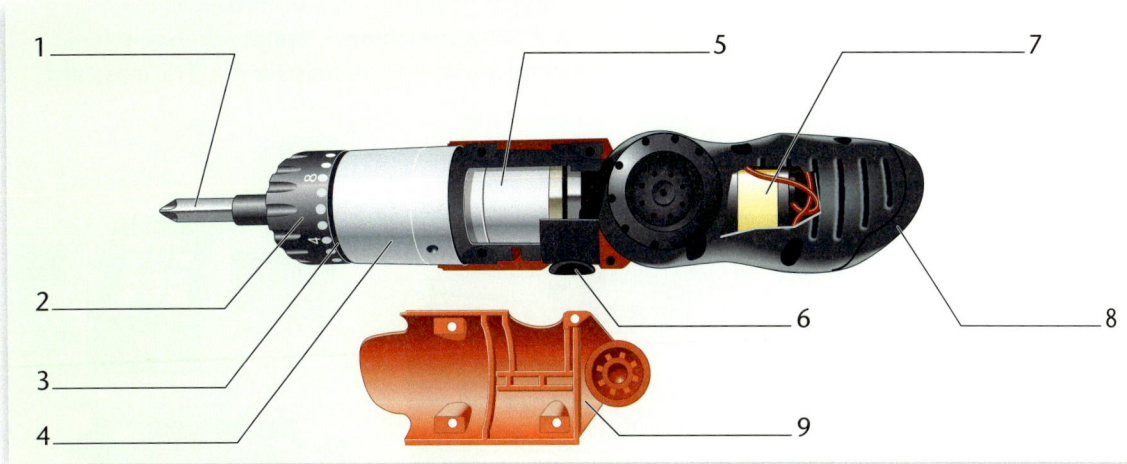

1 _____

2 _____

3 _____

4 _____

5 _____

6 _____

7 _____

8 _____

9 _____

T7 **4** **Complete the text on planetary gears with words or expressions from the list below. Then listen to the CD to check your answers and fill any gaps.**

drive shaft • 56 times • metal • motor • planetary gear • planets • reduction ratio • ring gear • screwdriver • screws • sun gear • torque

Technically, the most interesting feature of a power _____ [1] is that it reduces the fast spin of a relatively small electric _____ [2] to the incredibly high torque or 'twist' of the screwdriver bit. This _____ [3] is sufficient to drive _____ [4] into wood and _____ [5] without difficulty. How is this done? It is achieved by means of two linked _____ [6] systems, one of which you can see below.

The _____ [7] is connected to the _____ [8] of the motor. The sun gear turns three planetary gears or '_____' [9] connected to the outer _____ [10]. The gear system has a _____ [11] of 56:1. This means that the motor shaft rotates _____ [12] for the chuck to rotate just once, thus converting 'spin' into torque.

Ring gear

Planet

Sun gear

Planet

Machine tools

1 Label the machine tools with an expression from the list. One of them has no photo. Which one?

centre lathe • milling machine • metal-shearing machine • column drill • metal press • CNC lathe • punching machine • CNC-Drehmaschine • Metallpresse • Schermaschine • Spitzendrehmaschine • Ständerbohrmaschine • Stanzmaschine • Fräsmaschine

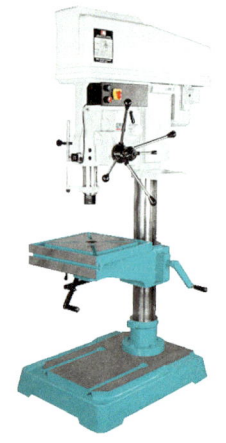

1 _____

2 _____

3 _____

4 _____

5 _____

6 _____

2 Which machines are used in the production of the following products?

1 hinge

2 sheet steel profiles

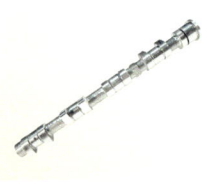

3 camshaft

4 colander

5 car door panel

T 8 **3** Listen to the description of a typical column drill and label the parts with words or expressions from the list.

base • chuck • column • depth gauge • drill bit • quill drive • feed lever • locking clamp • motor • pulley safety guard • switch • table

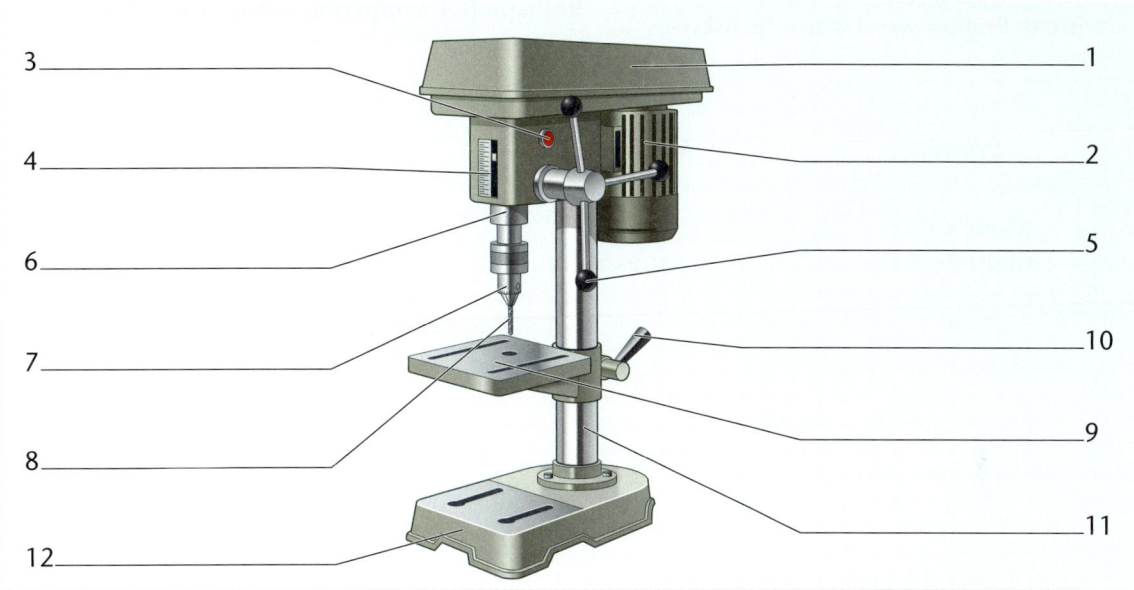

3_____

4_____

6_____

7_____

8_____

12_____

1_____

2_____

5_____

10_____

9_____

11_____

T 9 **4** First, try to complete the text with words from the list. Then listen to the CD to check your answers and fill any gaps.

a) column drill • b) drive • c) easier to use • d) electricity • e) grinders • f) guide • g) hand tools • h) machine tools • i) manual power tools • j) mobility • k) muscle power • l) operator • m) portable • n) power tools • o) tools • p) workpiece

We divide _____¹ into two main groups, _____² and _____³. As the name suggests, a hand tool is operated by hand and is driven by '_____'⁴. A power tool, on the other hand, makes use of an external energy source, usually _____⁵ or compressed air. Because the user does not have to _____⁶ the tool himself, power tools are generally more precise and _____⁷ than hand tools. We divide power tools into two further groups, namely _____⁸ and machine tools. In metalworking, the first of these two groups is made up of tools like drills, _____⁹ and metal saws. Although these tools are powered by an external energy source, the operator must still support and _____¹⁰ the tool by hand. Machine tools – a _____¹¹ or a centre lathe, for example – are quite different because they both hold the _____¹² in place and guide the cutting edge. All the _____¹³ has to do is set up and supervise the machine. A further difference is the _____¹⁴ of tools. Manual power tools, like hand tools, are _____¹⁵ so the operator can take the tool to the workpiece. But in the case of _____¹⁶ the workpiece must be taken to the tool.

Metal processing

1 Read this overview of metal processing technology from bottom to top. Replace the German words with an English word from the list.

bending • ~~casting~~ • Coating • cutting • drilling • galvanizing • glueing • grinding • Joining • painting • pressing • punching • Reshaping • tempering/annealing • welding

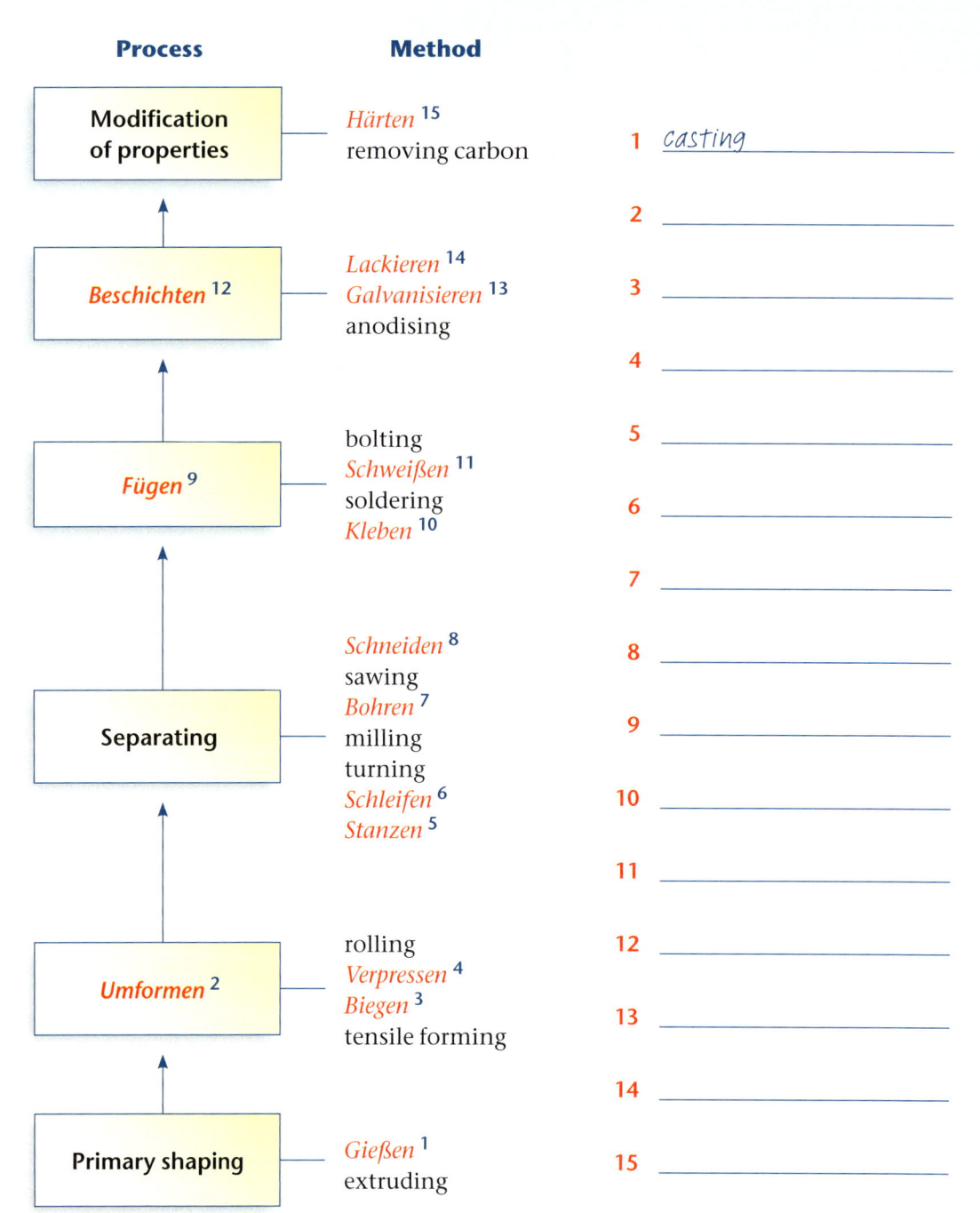

Process	Method	
Modification of properties	*Härten* 15 removing carbon	1 casting
		2
Beschichten 12	*Lackieren* 14 *Galvanisieren* 13 anodising	3
		4
Fügen 9	bolting *Schweißen* 11 soldering *Kleben* 10	5
		6
		7
Separating	*Schneiden* 8 sawing *Bohren* 7 milling turning *Schleifen* 6 *Stanzen* 5	8
		9
		10
		11
Umformen 2	rolling *Verpressen* 4 *Biegen* 3 tensile forming	12
		13
		14
Primary shaping	*Gießen* 1 extruding	15

2 Put the illustrations A–F into the order (1–6) of the manufacturing process. Then label the illustrations with a word or expression from the list.

> painting • casting • tempering / annealing • welding • deep-drawing / pressing • shearing

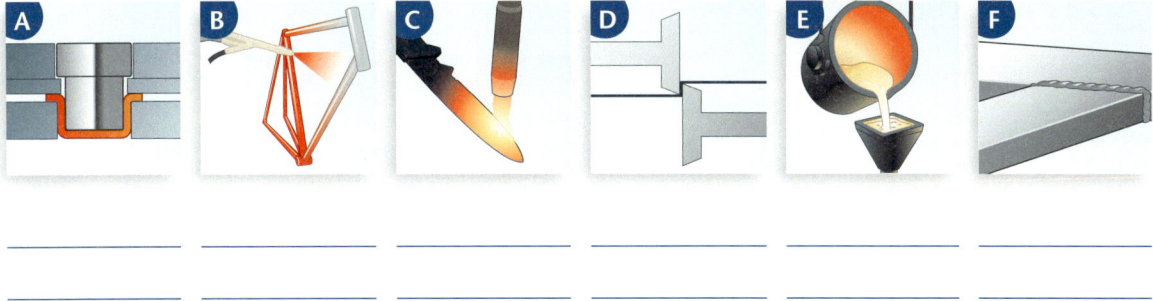

A   B   C   D   E   F

_____ _____ _____ _____

_____ _____ _____ _____

T 10 **3** First, try to complete the text on drop forging with words or expressions from the list. Then listen to the CD to check your answers and fill in any gaps.

> advantage • cast • complex • crankshaft • die • drop forging • finished product • forging • hammer • improves • machine • metal • metal workers • objects • plates • press • strength • workpiece

The oldest type of forging is beating red hot _____ [1] with a heavy

_____ [2]. But while this method of _____ [3]

is fine for making flat _____ [4] like knives and _____ [5],

it is also very limited. Then _____ [6] found that they could

make more _____ [7] shapes by hammering the hot metal into a _____ [8] containing

the 'mirror image' of the _____ [9]. Modern forging makes use

of either a falling hammer – hence the expression '_____ [10] –

or a hydraulic ram to _____ [11] the hot metal into dies positioned above and below

the _____ [12]. The _____ [13] of drop forging is that it

improves the _____ [14] of the metal by aligning and stretching its internal structure.

There are two ways of manufacturing a metal object – a _____ [15], for example.

One way is to _____ [16] it from molten metal. Another way is to _____ [17] it from

a larger block of metal. But the problem is that neither of these methods _____ [18]

the internal structure of the workpiece.

Cutting metals

1 Link the photos of standard metal forms to the correct labels.

aluminium sheet • hex(agonal) bar • rod • round bar • steel plate • square bar • tube • wire

 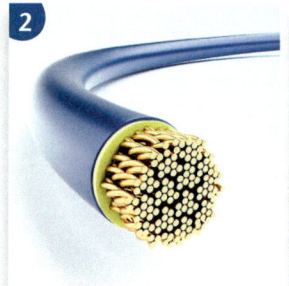  

_____ _____ _____ _____

_____ _____ _____ _____

2 Write down the name of the product and the metal form it is made from.

bolts • disposable plate • safe • soap dish • flat washers • drill bits

1 _____

2 _____

3 _____

4 _____

5 _____

6 _____

T11 **3** Alan Davis works for an engineering company in Birmingham. Here, he is showing some first-year trainees a waterjet cutter. Listen to the CD and link the sentence parts to make true statements.

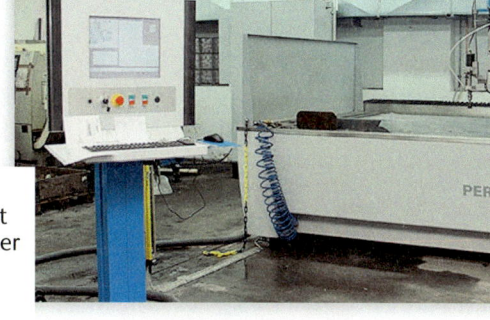

Inlet water

Jewel

waterjet cutter

1 In Alan's company, waterjet
2 Pure waterjet cutters use only water
3 Inlet water passes down a pipe
4 At the cutting head, the pressurised water
5 Nozzles are not made of metal,
6 Metal nozzles wear away quickly
7 If a medium doesn't lose its form under stress,
8 The water jet in a waterjet cutter is

A but of a very hard jewel.
B cutters are used to cut metal.
C is forced through a very fine nozzle.
D more like a knife than a stream of water.
E at very high pressure.
F under the pressure of water.
G we say that it is 'coherent'.
H without any additives.

1 ____   2 ____

3 ____   4 ____

5 ____   6 ____

7 ____   8 ____

Saying large numbers
Say the numbers – also double numbers, e.g. **55** – one after the other.
In technical contexts, use *zero* (**0**) for a nought (**0**):
18995006: one – eight – nine – nine – five – zero – zero – six

Saying decimals
Say the numbers one after the other. Use **point**, never ~~comma~~!
4092.75: four – zero – nine – two **point** seven – five

T12 **4** Here is Alan Davis again with some of the technical specifications of the waterjet cutter. Listen carefully and complete the sentences with the missing values.

1 With soft metals like copper, the water pressure through the nozzle is about _____ bar.

2 The air pressure in a very hard bicycle tyre is around _____ bar.

3 For cutting hard metals like tungsten steel, the water pressure can be as high as _____ bar.

4 The diameter of the nozzle hole is between _____ centimeters

and _____ centimeters.

5 In Alan's machine, water passes through the nozzle at more than _____ km/hr,

but some modern cutters have water jet speeds of up to _____ km/hr.

6 Advanced machines can cut _____ cm-thick hard steel at a speed of

around _____ cm/min.

Shaping

1 Label the drawings 1–4.

In industrial applications, the main methods of shaping metal are bending, compressing, pressing, including rolling, extruding, turning on a lathe and, finally, casting (see Unit 11). The workpiece is usually – but not always – shaped when hot.

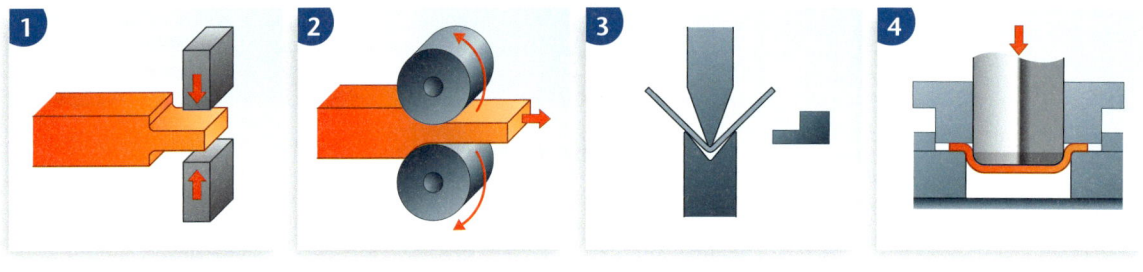

_____ _____ _____ _____

T13 2 Listen to the instructions for doing an experiment to prove that metal expands when heated. Then give the English equivalents of the highlighted German words or phrases.

Um diesen Versuch auszuführen, benötigen Sie[1] zwei leere Flaschen, einen Korken, eine Stricknadel aus Aluminium[2], eine hohe Kerze, einen Nagel aus Messing[3], einen schmalen Papierstreifen und Zündhölzer[4].

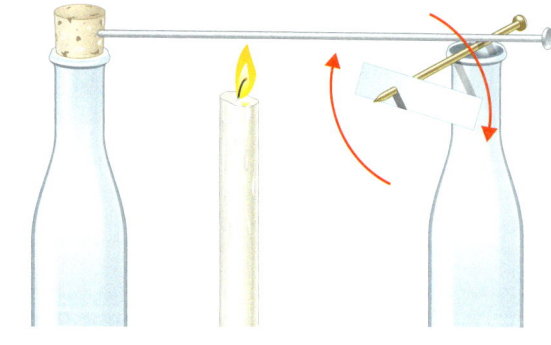

Drücken Sie den Korken[5] in die linke Flasche. Stechen Sie[6] das spitze Ende der Stricknadel in den Korken hinein und legen Sie das andere Ende der Stricknadel[7] auf die rechte Flasche. Stechen Sie den Nagel durch den Papierstreifen und legen Sie ihn[8] dann unter die Stricknadel, wie in der Zeichnung. Stellen Sie die Kerze zwischen die beiden Flaschen,[9] und zwar direkt unter die Stricknadel, und zünden Sie die Kerze an[10].
Nach einer kurzen Weile dreht sich der Papierstreifen leicht nach rechts[11]. Der Grund? Die Stricknadel expandiert und bewegt den Nagel[12]. Wenn die Kerze entfernt wird, zieht sich die Stricknadel wieder zusammen[13] und der Papierstreifen bewegt sich zurück in seine ursprüngliche Position[14].

1 _____	8 _____
2 _____	9 _____
3 _____	10 _____
4 _____	11 _____
5 _____	12 _____
6 _____	13 _____
7 _____	14 _____

3 Label the photos with the correct caption.

An aluminium window profile •
An aluminium window frame •
aluminium tubes

_____   _____   _____

_____   _____   _____

4 Read the description of the aluminium extrusion process and label the drawing of an extrusion press.

The first step in the aluminium extrusion process is to heat an aluminium billet – that can weigh anything up to 48kg – to a temperature of approximately 500°C in a furnace.

While in a hot malleable state, the billet is placed in a steel container (red component) and pushed through a steel die held in place by a tool container (right-hand blue component). This is done by means of the main ram (left-hand blue component) pushed forward by hydraulic pressure from the hydraulic chamber (left-hand green component). The main ram is capable of exerting a pressure of over 1600 tonnes on the billet via the ram head (pink component). The billet is forced through the steel die, emerging as aluminium profile.

The emerging profile is cooled as it is guided along a runout table. It is then subjected to a stretching process to straightens it. Finally the profile is cut to the length specified by the customer and may then go through a further heat treatment operation, depending upon the properties required.

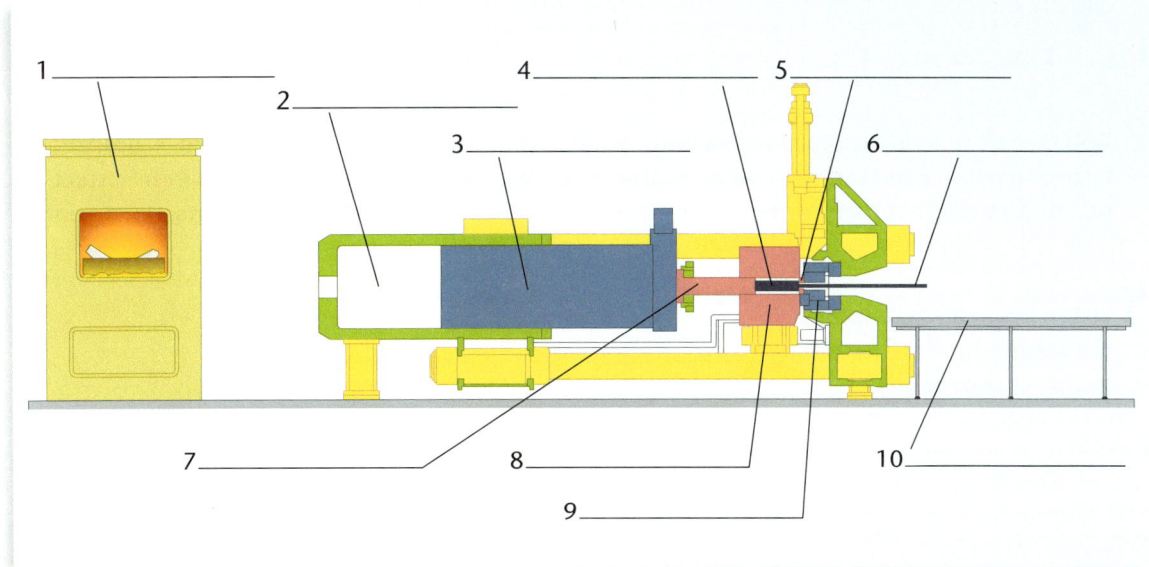

Casting

1 Link the drawings 1–4 to the correct explanatory texts,
A–D. Then fill in captions from the list.

Rotocasting • Pressure casting •
Permanent-mould casting •
Break-mould casting

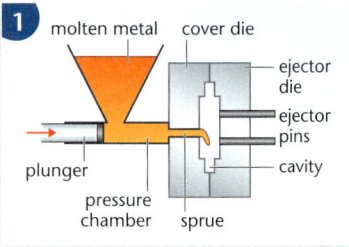

1
molten metal   cover die
ejector die
ejector pins
cavity
plunger
pressure chamber   sprue

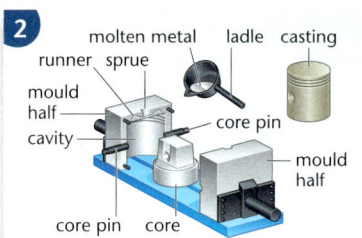

2
molten metal   ladle   casting
runner   sprue
mould half
cavity
core pin
mould half
core pin   core

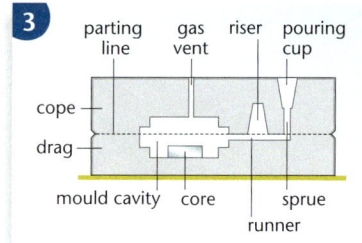

3
parting line   gas vent   riser   pouring cup
cope
drag
mould cavity   core   sprue
runner

_____ _____ _____

_____ _____ _____

A This kind of casting uses a mould made of hardened
foundry sand bonded with oil. The molten metal is poured
into the sprue through the pouring cup and then passes
along the runner into the mould. It is only used once
because the sand mould has to be broken to remove the
casting.

B The mould is in the form of a metal die. Molten metal is
forced into the cavity under pressure. This method of
casting is fast and is used for complicated shapes.

C In this type of casting, molten metal is poured into a mould
that is rotating at high speed (300 to 3000 rpm). The metal
is thrown outwards into the surrounding cavity. This
casting method is used to manufacture pipes and other
cylindrical shapes.

D The mould separates into two halves so that the casting can be removed easily. With this
casting method, the mould can be used again up to 100,000 times.

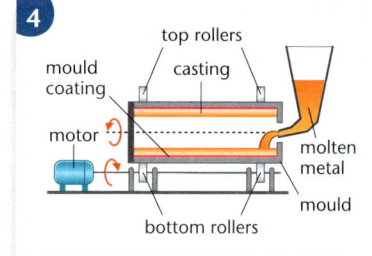

4
top rollers
mould coating   casting
motor
molten metal
mould
bottom rollers

_____

_____

1 _____ 2 _____ 3 _____ 4 _____

T 14 **2** Bob Garner is an instructor in a training workshop at a foundry.
Listen to the CD and put the metals in the list in the order in
which they are first mentioned.

aluminium • bronze •
copper • iron • steel •
tin • tungsten • zinc

3 Listen again and complete
the table with the melting
points of the metals.

Metal	Melting point
high-carbon steel	1 _____°C
iron	2 just above _____°C
low-carbon steel	3 _____°C
tin	4 _____°C
tungsten	5 _____°C
zinc	6 _____°C

4 Read the text and put in paragraph headings from the list . Which three paragraphs would you illustrate with the photos below?

1 _____

If you think that manufacturers are the biggest users of castings, you're right. If you think that they also use the biggest castings, then you're wrong. That honour goes to sculptors like Henry Moore. The discovery of bronze was a big leap forward. This alloy of copper and tin melts at around 900°C and has a low viscosity when molten.

2 _____

Firstly, bronze is much stronger and harder than pure metals like copper, lead and tin. This means that it can support great weights and can also be ground to make the cutting edges of knives snd cutting tools, for example. Secondly, bronze is very corrosion-resistant, which makes it ideal for use in shipbuilding and for outdoor applications.

3 _____

It's not surprising that sculptors soon saw the advantages of the new alloy. The strength and low viscosity of bronze made it possible to produce big, free-standing statues like the one of Marcus Aurelius in Rome.

4 _____

If you look at a large stone or marble statue, you'll see that the subject is always sitting, lying down or leaning against something, as in the famous statue of Abraham Lincoln in Washington DC. This is because, unlike bronze, stone and marble cannot carry the weight of the statue without extra support.

5 _____

Sculptors who make big statues in bronze are really more like architects or even engineers than artists. First, they make detailed drawings and specifications of the sculpture. Often, they also make a model of the finished shape in clay or plasticine. They work closely with the foundry technician at all stages of production, particularly with mould-makers and metallurgists.

6 _____

Sculptors go to the foundry to supervise the assembly of sculptures which consist of several parts. And they also always carry out their own finishing work such as grinding and polishing. Large sculptures (like Henry Moore's in Bonn) are transported in sections and assembled on site. One thing a sculptor always does, though, is to make sure that all specifications and moulds are destroyed after casting.

Abraham Lincoln

Large two forms, Bonn

Marcus Aurelius, Rome

Advantages of bronze for large statues • Assembly and finishing • Discovery of bronze • Production process • Useful properties of bronze • Weakness of stone for large statues

Fixing devices

1 Read the text and make two lists,
a) fixing devices (up to 9 items), and
b) devices which lock them in position
(up to 8 items).

Bolts are used either with removable nuts or screwed directly into a drilling (a threaded hole) in a workpiece. A stud is a bolt without a head. One end is screwed into a drilling, the other end is used with a nut.

For non-moving parts we generally use flat washers beneath the head of the bolt or its nut to protect the workpiece.

With moving parts, we use a locking device such as a spring washer or a tooth washer to stop the bolt or nut from becoming loose. We can increase reliability by using a lock nut, or a castle nut with a split pin or locking wire. A tab washer also keeps bolts or nuts tight.

Hex bolts have a six-sided head that is turned with a spanner or socket wrench. They are relatively easy to turn, come in many sizes, can withstand high torque and can be reused several times. On the other hand, hex nuts and bolts need a lot of space because tools are positioned around their outer faces.

Hex socket bolts are turned with an Allen key and they can be placed close together where space is limited. They are also available with a countersunk head that is flush with the workpiece. On the other hand, socket bolts are not as easy to turn as hex bolts are, and they cannot withstand as much torque.

For permanent fixings, rivets, welded joints or adhesives are generally used instead of nuts and bolts. Low-stress, non-moving parts are often fixed with self-tapping screws.

Fixing devices:

bolt, _____

Locking devices:

_____

2 Complete the sentences with words or expressions from the wordfields you have collected in exercise 1 above.

1 A _____ stops nuts and _____ from becoming loose.

2 A _____ has a hole through it to take a split pin or a _____.

3 _____ can be placed closer together than hex bolts can.

4 As the name says, a _____ cuts its own hole in thin material.

5 One end of a _____ is screwed into a drilling and the other end is used

   with a _____.

6 A _____ is pushed through a hole and then its end is deformed to hold it in place.

3 Link the sentence parts to make true statements about fixing and locking devices.

1 Bolts are used with nuts or
2 Engine cylinder blocks have drillings
3 One use of flat washers is to protect
4 Another advantage of washers is that they
5 We use locking devices with moving parts
6 Castle nuts with split pins are a very
7 As a rule, the space available determines
8 Countersunk bolts are used if the bolt head

A good way of holding nuts securely in place.
B make it easier to remove fixing devices.
C must be flush with the workpiece.
D the workpiece when nuts are turned.
E they are screwed into drillings.
F to stop nuts and bolts from loosening.
G whether to use hex or hex socket bolts.
H with studs for the cylinder head.

4 Work with a partner. Read the speech bubbles and then ask and answer questions about the devices in the grid. Swap roles at least once.

castle nut • countersunk bolt • drilling •
external tooth washer • flat washer • hex nut and bolt •
hex socket bolt • internal tooth washer • lock nut •
locking wire • rivet • self-tapping screws •
split pin • spring washer • stud • tab washer

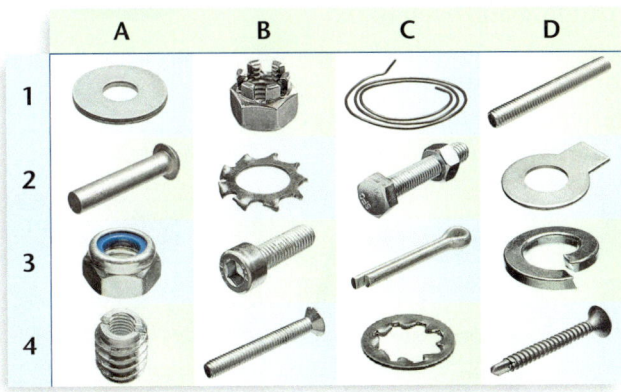

What's the fixing device in square A1?

It's a flat washer.

Can you find a flat washer?

Sure. There's one in square A1.

T 15 5 Work with a partner. First, read the sentences. Then listen to the telephone enquiry and fill in the missing details.

1 _____ of Albion Motorcycles is calling _____ of Fixing Solutions Limited.

2 Pete's firm is enquiring about _____ to fix an aluminium sidecar to a _____.

3 Specifically, Pete is looking for high-carbon steel nut and hex _____.

4 The bolt should have an overall length of _____ cm with a thread length of at least _____ cm.

5 Ben goes on to ask _____ about _____ to protect the fixing from stress

and _____.

6 Pete says that his firm is thinking of using a _____ under

the bolt head to secure the fixing, but Ben thinks a _____

under a _____ with a _____ would be

safer.

Industrial adhesives

1 Read the text and label the photos with the English equivalents of the German words. Then say which two components cannot be assembled with an adhesive, and why.

'Bonding' is joining parts without the help of a fixing device such as nuts and bolts, but by chemical means. The two most common types of chemical bonding are welding (see Unit 14) and using an adhesive, mainly polyurethane epoxies and glassy matrix epoxies.

The best locations for using adhesives are ones where the main forces exerted on the components are compression, i.e. pushing together, or shearing, where the force tries to slide the joined surfaces against one another.

This is why a number of non-moving engine parts such as valve covers are often fixed with just a few locating screws and adhesives that act as both a fixative and a sealant. They are also used for non-opening rear windows, airbag retainers, sound insulation, padding and even to fix body panels to the platform.

However, current adhesives are not suitable for use with turning or rotating components such as disc brakes or starters, for example. This is because they have a very low resistance to rotational forces.

Anlasser

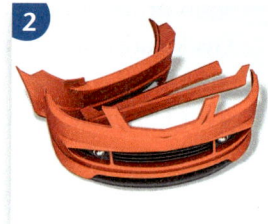

Karosserieteile

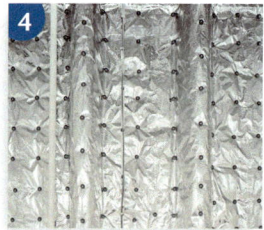

Ventilhaube   *Schalldämmung*   *Heckscheibe*   *Scheibenbremse*

■ The two components that cannot be assembled with adhesives are the _____ [1] and the _____ [2]. This is because adhesives have a _____ [3] to _____ [4].

2 Look at the photos and listen to the CD. Then choose the correct answer, a), b) or c).

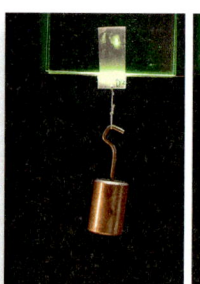

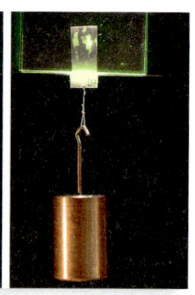

Gecko lizard   **Gecko's foot**   **Area of adhesion of gecko tape**

1   Geckos are a kind of **a)** adhesive, **b)** frog, **c)** lizard.
2   Geckos' feet enable them to **a)** climb very fast, **b)** hang upside down, **c)** jump big distances.
3   A gecko's glue is so strong that it can **a)** catch and hold other animals, **b)** hold its own weight upside down, **c)** support its own weight plus a further 40kg.
4   British scientists have developed **a)** an adhesive tape, **b)** an expoxy adhesive, **c)** a polymer adhesive called Synthetic Gecko.
5   Scientists in California have now used gecko glue to make **a)** adhesive tape, **b)** a liquid adhesive for industrial applications, **c)** even stronger adhesives.
6   A useful property of gecko tape is that the area of adhesion changes in proportion to the **a)** amount of weight to be carried, **b)** kind of material it is applied to, **c)** temperature.
7   Although scientists are developing even stronger adhesives, gecko glue **a)** has a unique combination of properties, **b)** is easier to produce than other adhesives, **c)** is ecologically safer than other adhesives.
8   Gecko adhesive maintains its adhesive power **a)** at any temperature, **b)** on rough and dirty surfaces, **c)** on wet surfaces.

1 ____   2 ____   3 ____   4 ____   5 ____   6 ____   7 ____   8 ____

3 **Read the product description and then complete the text.**

E-6000 industrial adhesive

E-6000 industrial adhesive can meet virtually any maintenance need. This multi-purpose, one component, self-levelling adhesive and sealant is so versatile that it practically eliminates the need for any other glue, epoxy, silicone, rubber cement or repair kit.

SUPERIOR STRENGTH AND VERSATILITY

- First, E-6000 is possibly the strongest and toughest adhesive and sealant available for industrial applications. But although E-6000 has a very high tensile strength, it also remains extremely flexible, even when used underwater. This elasticity makes E-6000 ideal when used as an adhesive or sealant between surfaces with different expansion coefficients.

- While strength is important, versatility is E-6000's most unique feature. Quite possibly, it is the only adhesive and sealant that will bond to all these different porous and non-porous substrates: metal, wood, plastic, tile, glass, fibreglass, concrete, brick, rubber, canvas, leather, vinyl and textiles.

- Furthermore, E-6000 can be applied to both oil and water-based paints, or it can be painted over by both of these. And finally, E-6000 is extremely non-corrosive, and except for a few high-powered solvents, may be used in contact with most chemical substances and solutions.

First, E-6000 has very high _____ [1] and extreme _____ [2], even under water.

Secondly, its _____ [3] means it can _____ [4] almost any combination of both porous

and _____ [5] materials. Thirdly, E-6000 can be applied to and _____ [6]

with both oil-based and water-based _____ [7] and, finally, it is _____ [8] when

exposed to almost all _____ [9] substances, except for a few high-powered _____ [10].

Welding and soldering

1 Label the drawings with highlighted words from the text.

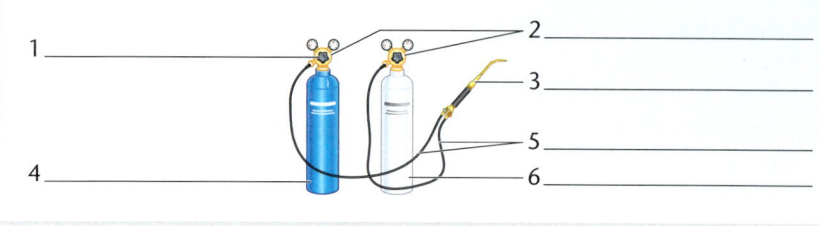

1 _____
2 _____
3 _____
5 _____
4 _____
6 _____

Oxyacetylene welding equipment consists of two cylinders, a yellow or white **acetylene cylinder** and a blue or green **oxygen cylinder**, joined by means of two flexible rubber **hoses** to the **welding torch**. The cylinders are fitted with **pressure regulators** to reduce the pressure in the cylinders to the much lower torch pressure. Each cylinder has a **cylinder valve** to turn the gases on or off.

The gases must be supplied to the welding torch at low pressure to produce a suitable flame. In typical welding processes, oxygen is supplied at 2.5 bar and acetylene at 0.25 – 0.5 bar in a ratio of 1:1. When the torch is ignited, the acetylene is turned on first. Oxygen is then added to the relatively cool acetylent flame to bring it up to a working temperature of approximately 3200°C. The 1:1 mix produces a neutral flame, i.e. a flame without excess oxygen or acetylene in it. Neutral flames are used in most welding processes in manufacturing and construction industries.

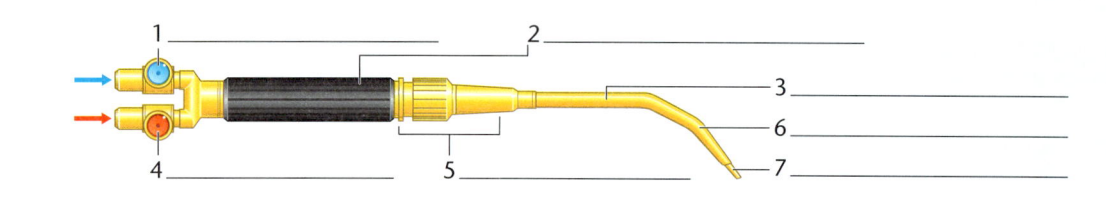

1 _____
2 _____
3 _____
6 _____
4 _____
5 _____
7 _____

The oxygen and the acetylene enter the welding torch through an **oxygen valve** (blue) and an **acetylene valve** (red). After passing through a pipe beneath an **anti-slip handle**, they mix in the correct 1:1 ratio in the **mixing chamber**. From there, the mixed gases enter the angled **head tube** and then pass through the **tip** of the torch to the **nozzle**.

2 Complete the statements with the missing details.

1 _____[1] cylinders are coloured blue or green, _____[2] cylinders yellow or white.

2 As _____[1] work most efficiently at low pressure, _____[2] reduce the pressure of gases in the cylinders.

3 Oxygen is supplied to the welding torch at a pressure of _____[1] and acetyline at 0.25 to _____[2] in a ratio of _____[3], which produces a _____[4].

4 The addition of _____[1] increases he temperature of the flame to about _____[2].

5 The oxygen and acetylene pass along separate _____[1] and are mixed in a _____[2] in the welding torch.

6 The gas mixture passes reaches the _____[1] through the _____[2] and tip.

3 Read the text and study the photos. Then answer the questions in your exercise book.

In a soldering process, metal parts are bonded by making the molten solder run into a joint and solidify. The solder has a melting point of below 400°C so that the metal parts themselves do not melt. After the metal cools, the joints are not as strong as the base metal, but have sufficient strength, electrical conductivity, and water-tightness for many applications, typically these:

printed circuits   electrical connections   pipe connections   metal seams

roof flashings   gutters   car radiators   jewellery

1 What is the main difference between soldering and welding?
2 How does a soldered joint differ from the base metal?
3 Which soldering applications require good electrical conductivity?
4 Which applications call for water-tightness?

4 Link the instructions a–f on how to solder copper pipes with rapid solder rings to the drawings 1–6.

a Apply flux to both pipe and fitting.
b Apply torch flame to base until solder emerges from fitting.
c Push pipe into fitting as far as ring and rotate.
d Clean end of pipe with emery cloth.
e Clean inside of fitting by wrapping emery cloth around finger.
f Insert ring into fitting.

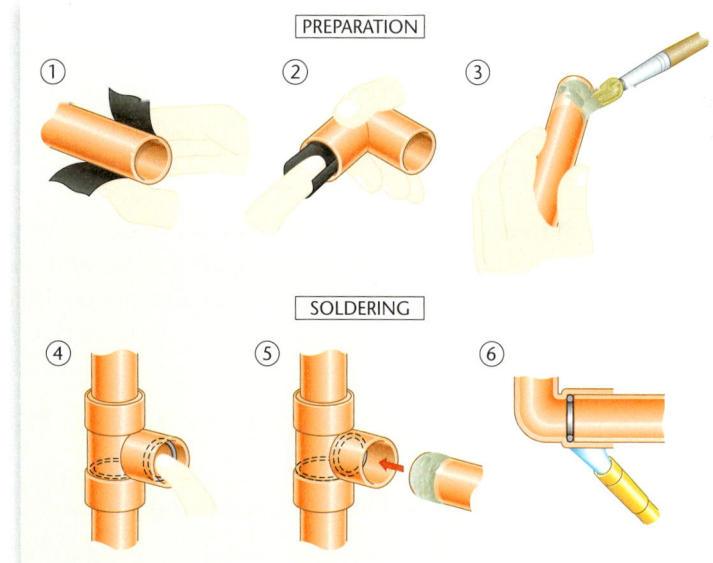

PREPARATION

SOLDERING

a ____ b ____ c ____ d ____ e ____ f ____

5 Listen to the radio report about a welding accident. Now listen again and make notes. Use your notes and write an accident report.

T 17

Friction and lubrication (Part 1)

1 Link the FAQs A–G to the answers 1–7. Then match the photos a–d to four of the answers.

1 In engineering, whenever two surfaces move against each other, there is always resistance to the movement. We call this resistance 'friction'. The amount of friction acting on a surface is called 'frictional force' (F_R).

2 We call the force needed to overcome frictional force 'displacement force' (F). The equation $F \geq F_R$ shows that the displacement force must be greater or equal to the frictional force to move surfaces over each other.

3 If the displacement force is smaller than the frictional force, the two surfaces do not move. We call this 'static friction', and it is what happens when you apply the brakes of a bike. The displacement force of the wheel rim is less than the frictional force of the brake pad, so static friction stops the wheel from turning.

4 In effect, 'normal forces' (F_N) are weight and gravity that also have an effect on the amount of friction acting on two surfaces.

5 The frictional coefficient (µ) combines the effects on movement of the materials themselves, their smoothness and the use of lubricants. It is measured on a scale from zero (very low) to 1.5+ (very high), and can only be found by trial and error. A piece of ice in a glass, for example, has a frictional coefficient of almost zero; a stationary car tyre on a road has a coefficient of around 1.4.

6 Once you have established the frictional coeffecient by trial and error, the frictional force acting on the contact area of two surfaces can be calculated by using the equation $F_R = µ \cdot F_N$..

7 When you drive a car, the displacement force of the tyre is greater than the frictional force of the road, so the car moves. We call this kinetic friction.

> **A** How can you calculate frictional force? • **B** What are 'normal forces'? •
> **C** What does 'displacement force' mean? • **D** What does 'frictional coefficient' mean? •
> **E** What is 'kinetic friction'? • **F** What is meant by 'friction' and 'frictional force'? •
> **G** What is 'static friction'?

1 ____ 2 ____ 3 ____ 4 ____ 5 ____ 6 ____ 7 ____ Photos: a ____ b ____ c ____ d ____

2 Answer the questions by filling in the missing words.

1 What does the equation $F \geq F_R$ tell us?

– It tells us that the _____ the frictional force (F_R).

2 Explain the equation $F_R = µ \cdot F_N$ in words.

– This equation means that the _____[1] multiplied by the

_____[2].

3 What happens when aircraft landing flaps are lowered?

– The frictional force created by _____[1] passing over the _____[2] is

less than the _____[3] force of the aircraft in flight, so the

aircraft continues to move owing to _____[4] friction. However, the

_____[5] slows the aircraft sufficiently for it to land safely.

3 The text about how disc brakes work is complete but the sentences are jumbled up. Use numbers from 1 to 7 to put them into the correct order and then label the drawing with the highlighted words or expressions.

____ This causes an increase in frictional force between the pads and the rotor sufficient to overcome the displacement force generated by the moving car.

____ The piston reduces the volume of the cylinder. This results in higher pressure in the **brake line** which is transmitted to the **piston** in the brake **calliper** by hydraulic oil.

____ The frictional force generated within the disc brake makes the car slow down and, if necessary, stop.

____ The pressure exerted by the oil on the piston presses the **brake pads** on to the **rotor** on the wheel **hub**.

____ In conclusion, we can say that disc brakes convert kinetic friction into static friction.

_1_ This is how a disc brake works.

____ When the **brake pedal** is pushed down, the driver's 'muscle power' is transmitted to the piston in the **master cylinder** through the **brake rod**.

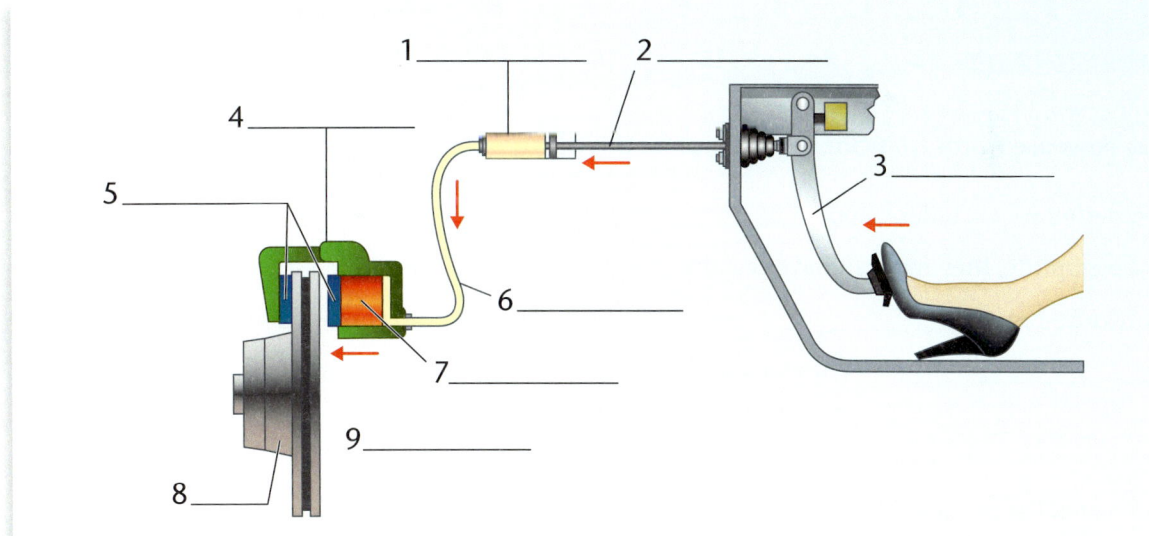

4 Listen to the 8 sounds of friction in action and link them to an item from the list a–h.

1 ____   2 ____   3 ____   4 ____

5 ____   6 ____   7 ____   8 ____

a) alpine skier • b) sandpaper on wood •
c) bird landing on water •
d) writing on blackboard •
e) in-line skater • f) rowing boat •
g) train stopping • h) violinist playing

T 18

Friction and lubrication (Part 2)

1 **Read the text and find the German equivalents of the highlighted words.**

a) Ablagerung • b) alterungsbeständig • c) beibehalten •
d) druckbeständig • e) Eigenschaften •
f) flüssiges Schmiermittel • g) Korrosion • h) Korrosionsstoffe •
i) Nebenwirkungen • j) nicht entzündbar • k) Ölwannenfilter •
l) Schleifteilchen • m) Temperaturbereich •
n) Trockenschmiermittel • o) Überschusshitze •
p) ungeschützte Teile • q) Verschleiß • r) Viskosität

The main function of lubricants is to reduce friction – and hence wear[1] – between moving surfaces. The parts are separated from each other by a thin film of liquid lubricant[2], usually a mineral oil or a synthetic oil, or by a layer of dry lubricant[3] such a graphite or, more recently, Teflon®.

However, lubricants also have some useful side-effects[4]. Firstly, they protect exposed parts[5] such as bicycle chains or hinges against corrosion[6]. Secondly, lubricants help to disperse excess heat[7] as in an internal combustion engine or when turning steel on a lathe, for example. As the oily black deposit[8] on an oil sump filter[9] shows, a third useful side-effect of liquid lubricants is to keep moving surfaces free of abrasive particles[10].

Lubricants need a variety of properties[11] to carry out these functions efficiently. They must be pressure-resistant[12], free of corrosive substances[13], adhesive at high temperatures and non-flammable[14]. They must have low frictional resistance and be able to maintain their viscosity[15] over a wide temperature range[16]. And, finally, they must be able to maintain[17] all these properties over long periods of continuous or frequent use. In other words, they must be ageing resistant[18].

1 ___ 2 ___ 3 ___ 4 ___ 5 ___ 6 ___ 7 ___ 8 ___ 9 ___ 10 ___

11 ___ 12 ___ 13 ___ 14 ___ 15 ___ 16 ___ 17 ___ 18 ___

2 **Now use words from above to complete this paragraph.**

Whether we are talking about _____[1] such as mineral oil or _____[2] like graphite, they must all have certain _____[3] in common. For example, they must be pressure-resistant, _____[4] and contain no corrosive substances or abrasive _____[5]. They should also be at least ageing resistant so that they maintain their _____[6] over long periods.

3 **Label the photos with words from the box.**

aeroengine • ball bearing • bike chain • boat screw • door lock •
gearbox • glass shelf • machine tool • ski-lift • snowmobile

 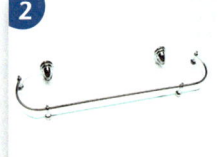   

_____ _____ _____ _____ _____

 6
 7
 8
 9
 10

_____ _____ _____ _____ _____

4 Read the table and say which oil would be most suitable for use in the applications shown in the photos in exercise 3.

Liquid lubricants

Type	Code	Properties, applications
Mineral oils	N	light oil without chemical additives for use in normal conditions, e.g. to lubricate locks, hinges, bicycle chains etc
	C	ageing restistant oil without chemical additives for bearings, gearboxes, differentials etc
	L	oils for chilling molten metals, tempering glass and cooling machine tools
Synthetic oils	PG	polyglycol oils with very low frictional resistance, ageing restistant, partly water-absorbant, useful for marine applications and severe weather applications, e.g. ski-lifts, snowmobiles
	SI	silicone oils for high temperatures, extremely water-resistant and ageing restistant, particularly suitable for aeroengines, high-speed trains etc

1 ____ 2 ____ 3 ____ 4 ____ 5 ____ 6 ____ 7 ____ 8 ____ 9 ____ 10 ____

T 19 **5** Listen to the CD and then a) label the drawing of the engine and b) use arrows to show the path of the oil in the engine.

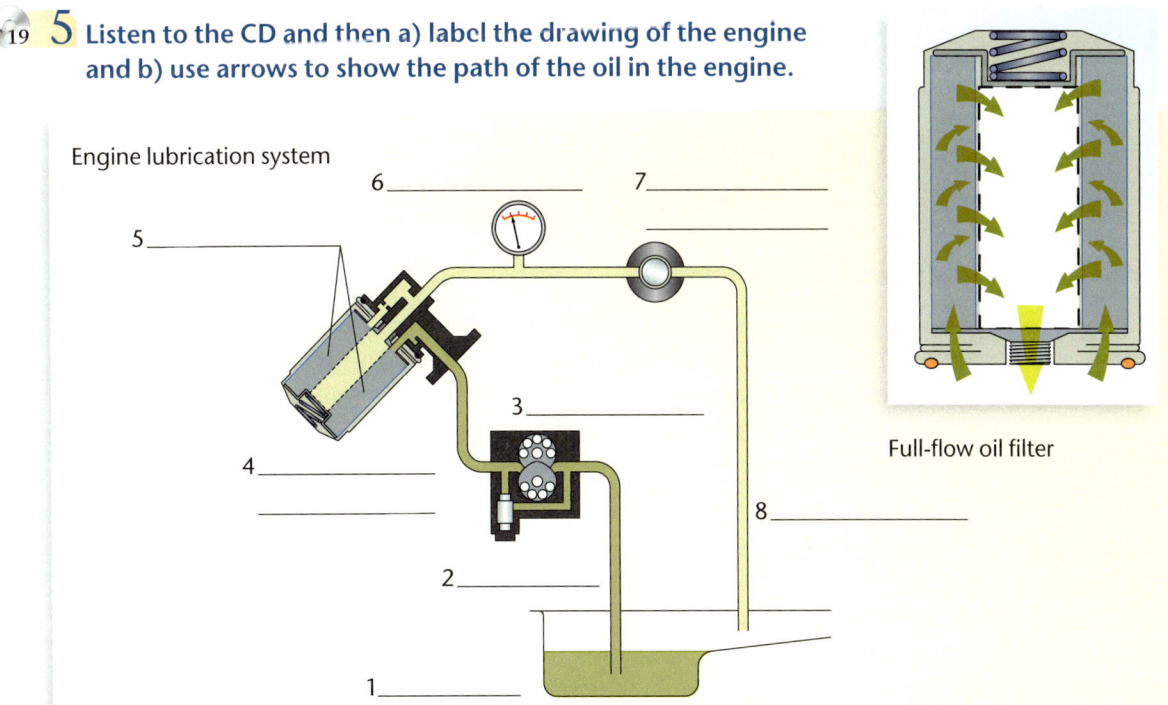

Engine lubrication system

5 _____
6 _____ 7 _____
_____
3 _____
4 _____
_____
8 _____
2 _____
1 _____

Full-flow oil filter

Corrosion

1 Mediation: Use the German prompts to talk about the photos in English.

Economists estimate that corrosion damage to transport infrastructure alone costs Germany around 10 billion* euros per year. By far the biggest and most expensive form of corrosion in metal is the rusting of iron and steel in moist air and salt water. Here are some examples:

* In technical contexts, 1 billion = one thousand million

railway lines   steel bridge   docks   crash barriers   traffic lights   road signs

Sie möchten jemandem sagen, dass …

1 … alle Fotos Korrosionsschäden an Verkehrsinfrastruktur zeigen.

_____ to transport infrastructure.

2 … es sechs Beispiele solcher Schäden gibt.

_____ damage.

3 … drei der Beispiele mit Straßen zu tun haben.

_____ .

4 … das erste Foto eine rostige Gleisanlage zeigt.

_____ .

5 … Seehäfen wie in dem dritten Foto vom Rost wegen Salzwasser besonders gefährdet sind.

_____ particularly at risk _____ .

2 Read the text and answer the questions.

Rust is the everyday name for iron oxide (Fe_2O_3). Iron oxide is common because iron (Fe) combines with oxygen (O) very easily. When a drop of water (H_2O = dihydrogen oxide) hits an iron or steel surface, two things occur almost immediately. Firstly, the water, a good electrolyte, combines with carbon dioxide (CO_2) in the air to form carbonic acid (H_2CO_3), an even better electrolyte. Secondly, as the acid forms and the iron dissolves, some of the water breaks down into its component substances, hydrogen (H) and oxygen.

The free oxygen and dissolved iron react with each other to form iron oxide. This reaction frees some electrons and they flow from the anode part of the iron flow to the cathode, which is generally another point on the piece of iron, causing the rust to spread. The chemical compounds found in liquids like acid rain, sea water and the spray from salted roads in winter make them better electrolytes than pure water, which acelerates the rusting process even faster. The sodium (Na) in salt acts as a highly efficient accelerant.

1 What are the scientific names of 'rust' and 'water'?

_____.

2 What three substances are needed to turn iron into iron oxide?

_____.

3 How is carbonic acid produced in the rusting process?

_____.

4 What happens to water when carbonic acid forms and iron dissolves?

_____.

5 What happens to free electrons from the anode?

_____.

6 Why does salt water cause rusting faster than pure water?

_____.

T 20 **3 Listen to the instructions for carrying out an experiment to show that iron and steel rust faster in salt water than in pure water. Then provide the missing details.**

- For the experiment you need these five things: four _____[1],

  four _____[2], _____[3],

  a jug of _____[4] and a _____[5].

- The labels on the glasses are:

6 ____ 7 ____ 8 ____ 9 ____

	Verb	Noun
1		estimation
2	damage	
3	corrode	
4	rust	
5		combination
6		requirement
7		occurrence
8	accelerate	

4 Complete the table with the missing verbs and nouns. They are all used in this unit.

5 Complete the sentences with a word from the table.

1 Iron and steel _____ when the come into contact with air and water.

2 The everyday name of iron oxide is _____.

3 The sodium in salt tends to _____ the rusting process.

4 Corrosion costs huge amounts of money because of _____ to the transport infrastructure.

5 Three things must be present for rusting to _____.

6 When hydrogen and oxygen _____, they form dihydrogen oxide or water.

Corrosion resistance

1 Use the dialogue guide to ask and answer questions about the materials used in the two cars.

In engineering, we speak of corrosion avoidance and corrosion resistance. Obviously, the cheapest way to avoid corrosion is to choose a material that does not corrode in the environment in which the product will be used. This means that you have to think about the corrosion characteristics of materials under various conditions.

1974 Opel Kadett

2009 Opel Astra

> What were wheels made of in the 1970s?

In the 1970s	aerials	were made of	aluminium alloy.
On the Kadett	air-intakes	are made of	chromium-plated metal.
On the Astra	bumpers		glass.
	door handles		moulded plastic.
	hub caps		painted pressed sheet
	light units		steel.
	logos		plastic-coated wire.
	radiator grills		plastic-coated steel.
	sills		pressed steel.
	wheels		rubber.
	windows		…
	windscreen wipers		

> They were made of pressed steel, I think.

> And nowadays?

2 Read the text and then say what type of corrosion-resistant covering has been used to protect the objects in the photos.

chromium • oil • paint • plastic • zinc

It is, of course, not possible to choose a material simply by thinking about its corrosion characteristics. Factors such as strength and cost also play a big role. You would not, for example, use gold to make a ship's anchor, although gold is heavy and corrosion-resistant even in seawater. Anchors are generally made of cast iron or steel and have to be protected with a corrosion-resistant coating. As a rule, the corrosion-resistant coating is a film of oil, a coat of paint, a layer of corrosion-resistant metal such as chromium or zinc, or a plastic powder coating. The process of coating one metal with another is called galvanizing, and that of coating a metal with plastic is called electrostatic powder coating. Because the moving parts of machines cannot be permanently coated, they are protected against corrosion by an oil film. Paint is generally used for easily accessible surfaces. Galvanizing and electrostatic coating is suitable for protecting non-accessible surfaces and for surfaces exposed to the weather.

1

wheelbarrow

2

dish drainer

3

tap

4

engine piston

5

car body

3 Read the text and do the mediation exercise.

There are two methods of zinc galvanizing. In electrogalvanizing, zinc from the anode is deposited on the cathode (the workpiece) in an electrolyte bath by electrolysis. In hot-dip galvanizing, an iron or steel workpiece is coated with zinc (Zn) by passing it through a bath of molten zinc at a temperature of around 460 °C. The pure zinc coating reacts with oxygen to form zinc oxide (ZnO). This further reacts with carbon dioxide (CO_2) to form a coating of zinc carbonate ($ZnCO_3$). Although electrogalvanizing results in a much stronger bond and thinner layer of pure zinc than hot-dip galvanizing does, its big disadvantage is that it is not suitable for mass production. For this reason, nowadays hot-dip galvanizing – which can handle a large number of workpieces in a continuous process – is more common. And although the dull grey coating of zinc carbonate is neither as attractive nor as strong an electrogalvanized coating, it is nonetheless strong enough to stop corrosion in most environments. Hot-dip galvanizing is widely used for metal roofing, heating and cooling ducts in buildings, crash barriers, fencing, automotive body parts and numerous consumer products such as metal buckets and containers.

Sie möchten jemandem auf Englisch sagen, dass …

1   … es zwei Methoden der Verzinkung gibt, die galvanische Verzinkung und die Feuerverzinkung.
2   … die galvanische Verzinkung, obwohl sie ein besseres Ergebnis ergibt, für die Massenproduktion ungeeignet ist.
3   … heutzutage die Feuerverzinkung die gängigste Methode ist, eine hohe Zahl von Werkstücken zu bearbeiten.
4   … die Feuerverzinkung eigentlich eine Beschichtung aus Zinkcarbonat ergibt.
5   … Zinkcarbonat zwar nicht so hart wie reines Zink, aber hart genug für die meisten Anwendungen ist.
6   … feuerverzinkte Stähle in der Herstellung von zum Beispiel Blechbedachung, Schutzplanken und vielen Konsumartikeln verwendet werden.

T 21   **4** **It's open day at Wessex Galvanizing Limited. Tom Davis is describing the hot-dip galvanizing process to some visitors. Listen to the CD and link the notes A-G to the locations in the drawing 1–7.**

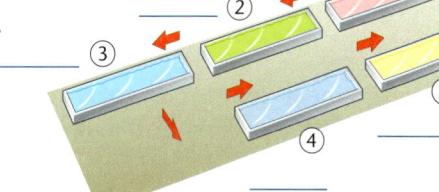

A Cooling or 'quenching' with chromate water • **B** Final storage before collection or delivery •
C Flux to remove oxides • **D** Hot caustic soda to remove oil etc •
E Inspection by quality control, weighing, packing • **F** Molten zinc bath, ca. 460°C •
G Pickling with hydrochloric acid to remove rust etc

Health and safety

1 Mediation: Explain to somebody who only understands German what the safety rules mean. The words in the list on the right will help you to do this.

PLANT SAFETY RULES

▸ WALK, don't run.
▸ KEEP STRICTLY TO the yellow walkways.
▸ USE pedestrian doors, NEVER swing-doors.
▸ NEVER TAP people on the shoulder from behind.
▸ KEEP your workplace clean and tidy.
▸ OBEY ALL safety signs at ALL times.
▸ MAKE SURE YOU KNOW what to do in an emergency.
▸ SEE and BE SEEN.

befolgen •
Fußgängertür •
gesehen werden •
halten • klopfen • Laufweg •
Notsituation • ordentlich •
Schulter • Schwingtür •
Sicherheitszeichen •
sich vergewissern

1 Die erste Regel schreibt vor, dass man laufen, aber nicht rennen soll.

2 Wir müssen uns an die _____ halten.

3 Wir dürfen nur die _____.

4 Die vierte Regel besagt, dass man nie _____ soll.

5 Die Leute sollten ihren _____.

6 Wir müssen _____ befolgen.

7 Die nächste Regel besagt, dass wir _____.

8 Die letzte Regel besagt, dass _____ muss.

2 Look at the signs and use the numbers 1 to 10 to say what they mean.

❶ ❷ ❸ ❹ ❺ ❻ ❼ ❽ ❾ ❿

Danger of high voltage [_] • Forklift trucks in use in this area [_] •
Hazardous biological waste [_] • Lethal toxic substance [_] • No pedestrians in this area [_] •
Wear a hard hat/safety helmet [_] • Use of mobile phones forbidden [_] •
Photography forbidden [_] • Wear protective ear muffs [_] • Wear protective gloves [_]

T 22 **3** You are about to hear descriptions of three safety signs. Listen to the descriptions and draw the signs. Work with a partner and make a rough sketch first.

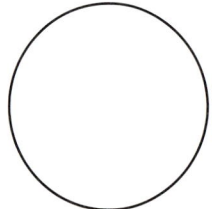 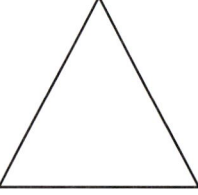 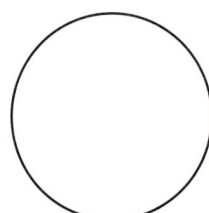

4 This American flowchart describes the safety procedures if fire breaks out in a manufacturing plant. Study the chart and then answer the questions in an exercise book.

According to the flowchart, what must you do …

1 … if the fire is quite big and not just in one place?
2 … if you have tried to put the fire out, but failed?
3 … if you have succeeded in putting out the fire?
4 … immediately after sounding the fire alarm?
5 … when you tell people to leave the area of the fire?

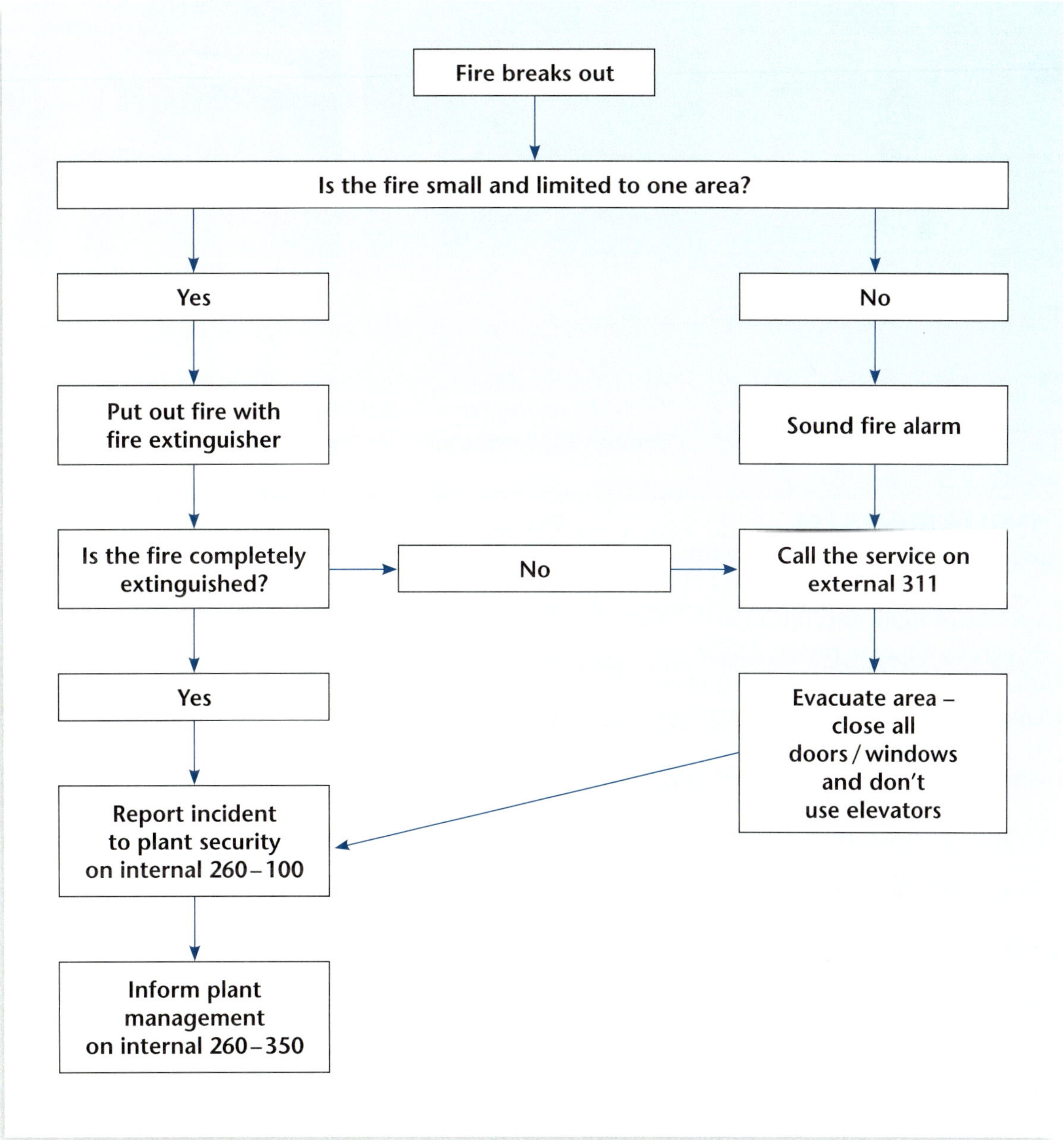

Fire breaks out

Is the fire small and limited to one area?

| Yes | No |

Put out fire with fire extinguisher

Sound fire alarm

Is the fire completely extinguished? → No → Call the service on external 311

Yes

Evacuate area – close all doors / windows and don't use elevators

Report incident to plant security on internal 260 – 100

Inform plant management on internal 260 – 350

Jobs

1 Use the letters to link the jobs in the list to the photos. Be careful. Two of the jobs do not fit at all.

A foundry worker • **B** lathe operator • **C** scaffolder • **D** steelmaker • **E** drill operator • **F** sheetmetal worker • **G** steel erector • **H** welder

1 ____ 2 ____ 3 ____ 4 ____ 5 ____ 6 ____

2 Read the job ads, the list of names and the statements. Say who is talking.

a) Fiona Hunter • **b)** Jeff Dixon • **c)** Jeff's assistant • **d)** Preston Steel manager • **e)** Scaffolder's wife • **f)** Site manager

ANGLIA HOMES Ltd

requires **SCAFFOLDERS** to work on sites in Cambridge and Huntingdon. Successful applicants must have at least 3 years recent experience, CSCS* qualifications and site safety training. Employers' references are also required. To apply, please submit CV to Fiona Hunter, Contracts Manager, Anglia Homes Ltd, 10-12 Newmarket Road, Cambridge, CB1 7TL.

Preston Steel Ltd

supplies fine steels of the highest quality to a wide variety of customers in the UK and abroad. Owing to our continued success, we are looking for experienced steelmakers to work at our Preston and Sheffield plants. Successful applicants will be offered permanent positions at top rates of pay. A bonus scheme is also in operation. If you are interested in an interview, please submit your CV to Jeff Dixon, Human Resources, at: **jeff.dixon@preston.co.uk.**

(* **CSCS** = Construction Skills Certification Scheme. Qualification awarded by experience, examination or both.)

- I have some good applicants, but they all want to work in Preston. **1** _____
- There's no way that I'm going to move to Cambridge. Just forget it! **2** _____
- We're expanding too fast. We'll never be able to fill these orders. **3** _____
- Mr Dixon would like you to come for an interview next Wednesday. **4** _____
- I'm sorry, but applicants must have at least three years experience. **5** _____
- Fiona, I need three more scaffolders. Can you help me? **6** _____

3 Read the letter below and complete the sentences with the missing details.

☞ There is no standard layout for business letters in English so you can use your usual style if you want. However, the **American full-block style** is popular because it is clear and very easy to use. The parts are simply listed in logical order on the left as in the example below.

(* **NVQ** = **N**ational **V**ocational **Q**ualification. **Level 3** is equivalent to the Gesellenbrief.)

1 The letter is from _____ to _____ of

   Bradford Castings Limited.

2 Ed found out about the job from an _____ in the _____.

3 Bradford Castings Ltd is looking for _____.

4 Ed wants a job because his present employer in _____ is moving to _____.

5 Ed has 7 years experience and an NVQ Level 3 qualification in _____.

24 Manor Road
Leeds
LS6 9FG

No full stop after day.

Tel. +44-(0)113-702115
Email ed.watson@fastnet.co.uk

22 May 20..

Attn = **Attention (z. H. v.)**

Bradford Castings Limited
50-52 Bolten Road
Bradford
BD8 3DD

If you don't know the person's name, use Dear Sir or Dear Madam. No comma!

Attn: Ms Sally Evans

Dear Ms Evans

I refer to your advertisement for foundry workers in the Leeds News of 20 May.

I am very interested in the job you advertise as my present employers in Sheffield are planning to move their foundry operations to Pakistan for cost reasons.

As you will see from the enclosed CV, I am experienced in all aspects of foundry work, including the assembly of molds, casting and grinding.
Before taking my present job three years ago, I worked at a foundry in Leeds for four years, during which time I obtained the NVQ Level 3* qualification in foundry technology.

I look forward to hearing from you in due course.

Yours sincerely

If you start with Dear Sir / Madam, sign off with Yours faithfully. No comma!

Ed Watson

Ens: CV

Enc / Encs = Enclosure(s)

T 23 **4** Listen to the telephone conversation between Ed Watson's wife, Annie, and Sally Evans of Bradford Castings Limited. Then complete Annie's telephone message to Ed.

Hi Ed,

I had to leave for work early today so I left you this note.

_____ ¹ of Bradford Castings called.

They want you to go for a job _____ ²!

The interview's at the _____ ³

in Bradford. The address is _____ ⁴.

Your interview's at _____ ⁵ on Wednesday,

_____ ⁶. I said I thought that would be all right

because you don't start work until _____ ⁷

that week. Okay? Oh, and can you confirm by email as soon as possible?

The e-mail address is _____ ⁸ See you later!

Love Annie

ANY OTHER STRENGTHS?

5 Read Harry Sutton's tips on how to write a CV and use them to write your own. Then swap your CV with a partner's. Any surprises?

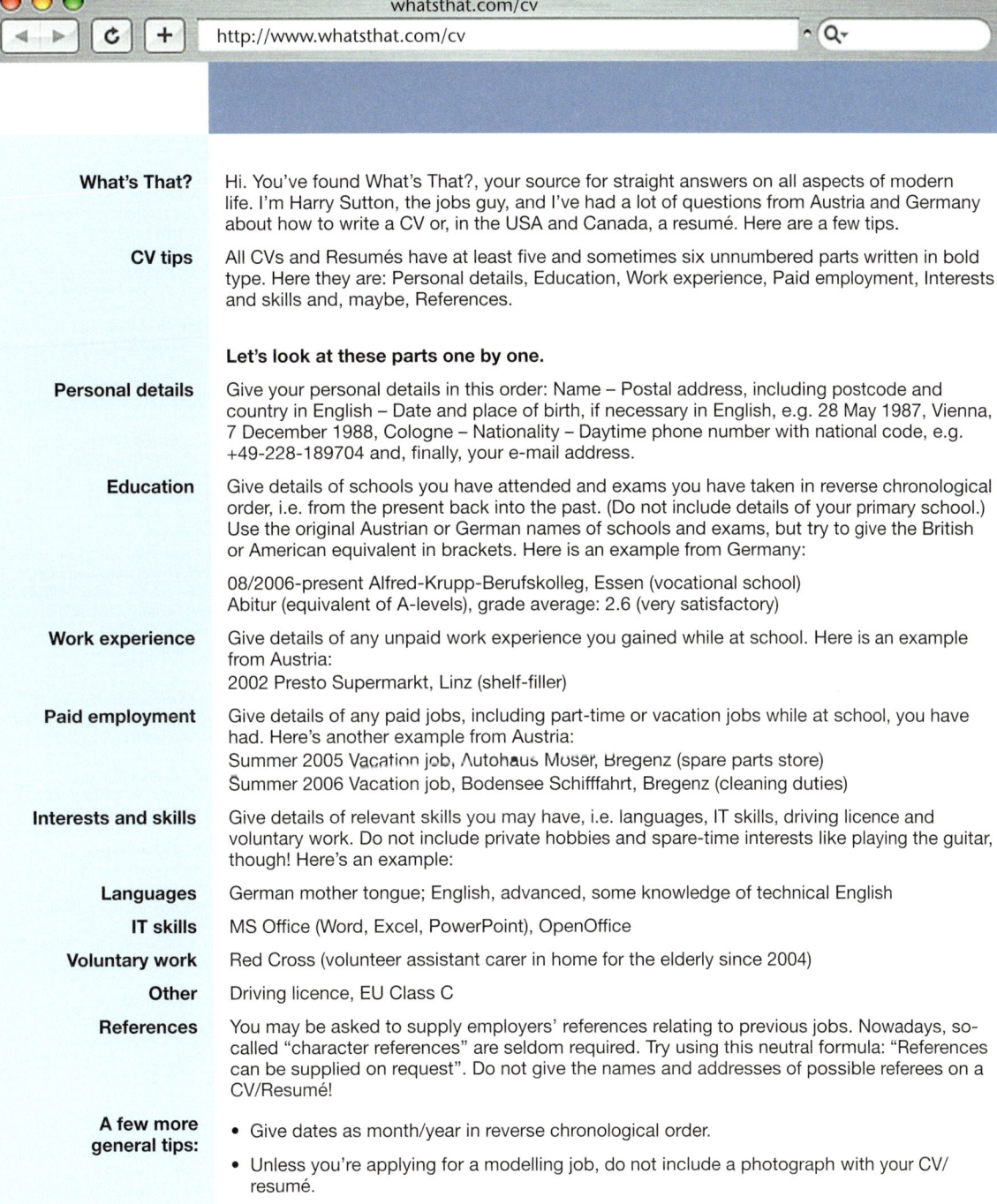

whatsthat.com/cv

http://www.whatsthat.com/cv

What's That?
Hi. You've found What's That?, your source for straight answers on all aspects of modern life. I'm Harry Sutton, the jobs guy, and I've had a lot of questions from Austria and Germany about how to write a CV or, in the USA and Canada, a resumé. Here are a few tips.

CV tips
All CVs and Resumés have at least five and sometimes six unnumbered parts written in bold type. Here they are: Personal details, Education, Work experience, Paid employment, Interests and skills and, maybe, References.

Let's look at these parts one by one.

Personal details
Give your personal details in this order: Name – Postal address, including postcode and country in English – Date and place of birth, if necessary in English, e.g. 28 May 1987, Vienna, 7 December 1988, Cologne – Nationality – Daytime phone number with national code, e.g. +49-228-189704 and, finally, your e-mail address.

Education
Give details of schools you have attended and exams you have taken in reverse chronological order, i.e. from the present back into the past. (Do not include details of your primary school.) Use the original Austrian or German names of schools and exams, but try to give the British or American equivalent in brackets. Here is an example from Germany:

08/2006-present Alfred-Krupp-Berufskolleg, Essen (vocational school)
Abitur (equivalent of A-levels), grade average: 2.6 (very satisfactory)

Work experience
Give details of any unpaid work experience you gained while at school. Here is an example from Austria:
2002 Presto Supermarkt, Linz (shelf-filler)

Paid employment
Give details of any paid jobs, including part-time or vacation jobs while at school, you have had. Here's another example from Austria:
Summer 2005 Vacation job, Autohaus Moser, Bregenz (spare parts store)
Summer 2006 Vacation job, Bodensee Schifffahrt, Bregenz (cleaning duties)

Interests and skills
Give details of relevant skills you may have, i.e. languages, IT skills, driving licence and voluntary work. Do not include private hobbies and spare-time interests like playing the guitar, though! Here's an example:

Languages
German mother tongue; English, advanced, some knowledge of technical English

IT skills
MS Office (Word, Excel, PowerPoint), OpenOffice

Voluntary work
Red Cross (volunteer assistant carer in home for the elderly since 2004)

Other
Driving licence, EU Class C

References
You may be asked to supply employers' references relating to previous jobs. Nowadays, so-called "character references" are seldom required. Try using this neutral formula: "References can be supplied on request". Do not give the names and addresses of possible referees on a CV/Resumé!

A few more general tips:
- Give dates as month/year in reverse chronological order.
- Unless you're applying for a modelling job, do not include a photograph with your CV/resumé.
- Do not exaggerate, particularly in relation to language skills. If your English is "just about satisfactory", don't say that it is "completely fluent".

Die Zahlen geben die Quelle des Wortes an, z. B. alloy *2.1* = Unit 2, Aufgabe 1

A

abrasive particles *16.1* – Schleifteilchen
accelerant *17.2* – Beschleuniger
(to) accelerate *17.2* – beschleunigen
accessible *18.2* – zugänglich
acetylene *14.1* – Acetylen
(to) act on *5.1* – wirken auf
additive *9.4* – Zusatz
adhesive *12.1* – Klebstoff
adjustable spanner *5.1* – verstellbarer Schraubenschlüssel
aerial *18.1* – Antenne
aeroengine graphite *16.3* – Flugmotorgraphite
ageing resistant *16.1* – alterungsbeständig
airbag retainer *13.1* – Airbagbehälter
aircraft landing flaps *15.2* – (Flugzeug-)Landeklappen
air-intake *18.1* – Luftschlitz
(to) align *8.3* – ausrichten
Allen key *5.1* – Inbusschlüssel, Innensechskantschlüssel
alloy *2.1* – Legierung
anchor *18.2* – Anker
angled *14.1* – abgewinkelt
anode *17.2* – Anode, positiver Pol
anodising *10.3* – das Eloxieren, elektrolytische Behandlung
anti-slip *14.1* – Gleitschutz
anvil *5.3, 8.4* – Amboss
applicant *20.2* – Bewerber/in
applications *1.1* – Anwendungen, Zwecke
(to) apply *20.2* – sich bewerben
approximately *10.4* – ungefähr, zirka
assembly *11.5* – Montage

B

ball-peen hammer *5.3* – Hammer mit Rundkopf und Pinne
bar *9.1* – Stab
base *7.3* – Fuß, Grundplatte
base metals *1.1* – unedle Metalle
(to) be capable of *10.4* – imstande sein
bearing *16.3* – Kugellager
bench vice (AE: vise) *5.1* – Bankschraubstock
bending *8.1* – das Biegen
bike chain *6.1* – Fahrradkette
billet *10.4* – Rohling
biological waste *19.2* – Biomüll
bit *6.3* – Bohrer
blacksmith *5.3* – Schmied
blast furnace *1.4* – Hochofen
block *8.3* – Block
boat screw *16.3* – Schiffsschraube
body panel *13.1* – Karosserieteil
bolt *5.2* – Bolzen, Schraube
bolt cutters *5.3* – Bolzenschneider
bond *18.3* – Verbindung
(to) bond (with) *11.1* – verbinden mit
brake calliper *15.3* – Bremslehre
brake line *15.3* – Bremsleitung, -schlauch
brake pad *15.1* – Bremsbelag
brake pedal *15.3* – Bremspedal
brake rod *15.3* – Bremsstab, -stange
brass *2.1* – Messing
break-mould casting *11.1* – Guss mit verlorenen Formen
brick *13.3* – Ziegel(stein)
brittle *4.3* – brüchig, spröde
bronze *11.5* – Bronze
bumper *18.1* – Stoßstange
bustle pipe *1.4* – Ringleitung für Heißluft

C

cable *5.3* – Kabel
(to) calculate *15.1* – berechnen
camshaft *4.2* – Nockenwelle
canvas *13.3* – Leinwand
capacity *2.1* – Kapazität, Fähigkeit

caption *3.3* – Bildunterschrift, -überschrift
car body *2.1* – (Auto-)Karosserie
carbon *2.1* – Kohlenstoff
car door panel *7.2* – Autotür
car radiator *14.3* – Autoheizung
car tyre *15.1* – Autoreifen
carbon dioxide *17.2* – Kohlendioxid
carbon steel *2.1* – Kohlenstoffstahl
carbonic acid *17.2* – Kohlensäure
(to) cast *8.3* – gießen
cast iron *1.4* – Gusseisen
casting *8.1* – Guss, das Gießen
castle nut *12.1* – Kronenmutter
cathode *17.2* – Kathode, negativer Pol
caustic soad *18.4* – Ätznatron
cavity *11.1* – Hohlraum
centre lathe *7.1* – Spitzendrehmaschine
chamber *10.4, 11.2* – Kammer
charging bell *1.4* – Beschickungsglocke, -kessel
chemical compound *17.2* – chemische Verbindung
chisel *4.2* – Meißel, Stemmeisen
chromate water *18.4* – chromsaures Wasser
chromium *18.1* – Chrom
chromium-plated *18.1* – verchromt
chuck *6.3* – Bohrfutter
chuck lock *6.3* – Bohrfutterarretierung
clay *11.5* – Ton, Lehm
coat of paint *18.2* – Farbschicht
coating *8.1* – Beschichtung, das Beschichten
coherent *9.4* – kohärent
coke *1.4* – Koks
colander *7.2* – Sieb
collection *18.4* – Abholung
column *7.3* – Säule
column drill *7.1* – Ständerbohrmaschine
combination *13.2* – Kombination
component *2.4* – (Bestand-)Teil
compressed air *7.4* – Druckluft
compressing *10.1* – das Komprimieren
compression *13.1* – Kompression, Druck
conclusion *15.3* – (Schluss)Folgerung
concrete *13.3* – Beton
conductivity *14.3* – Leitfähigkeit
conductor *1.1* – Leiter, integrierter Schaltkreis
construction industry *14.1* – Bauindustrie
consumer products *18.3* – Konsumartikel
continuous process *18.3* – laufender Prozess
contract *20.2* – (Arbeits-)Vertrag
(to) convert (into) *6.4* – umwandeln
conveyor *1.4* – Förderband
cooling duct *18.3* – Kühlleitung
copper *1.2* – Kupfer
(to) corrode *4.1* – korrodieren, rosten
corrosion *4.1* – Korrosion, Rostbildung
corrosion avoidance *18.1* – Korrosionsvermeidung
corrosion resistance *18.1* – Korrosionsbeständigkeit
corrosion-resistant *11.5* – rostfrei, korrosionsbeständig
corrosive substances *16.1* – Korrosionsstoffe
countersunk *5.2* – Senk(kopf)
countersunk head *12.1* – Senkkopf
cover *6.3* – Verkleidung
covering *18.2* – Verkleidung
crankcase *3.4* – Kurbelgehäuse
crankshaft *8.3* – Kurbelwelle
crash barrier *17.1* – Schutz-, Leitplanke
cross-cut head *5.2* – Kreuzschlitzkopf
cross-section *10.3* – Querschnitt
cutlery *1.1* – Besteck
cut-off saw *6.1* – Trennkreissäge
cutting edge *4.1* – Spitze, Schnittkante

cutting wheel *6.1* – Trennscheibe
cylinder block *2.1* – Zylinderblock
cylinder head *3.4* – Zylinderkopf
cylinder valve *14.1* – Zylinderventil

D

dead centre *3.4* – Scheitelpunkt, genauer Mittelpunkt
deep-drawing *8.2* – das Tiefziehen
(to) deform *12.2* – verformen
delivery *18.4* – (Aus-)Lieferung
deposit *16.1* – Ablagerung
depth *3.1* – Tiefe
depth micrometre *3.1* – Tiefen-Messschraube, Mikrometer
(to) destroy *11.5* – zerstören, vernichten
device *12.1* – Vorrichtung, Gerät
diameter *3.2* – Durchmesser
die (pl. dies) *8.3* – Pressstempel, -form
differential (gear) *16.4* – Differentialgetriebe
dihydrogen oxide *17.2* – Wasser
dimension *3.1* – Abmessung, Maß
dirt *3.3* – Schmutz
disc brakes *13.1* – Scheibenbremsen
displacement force *15.1* – Verdrängungskraft
disposable *9.2* – Einweg-, Wegwerf-
(to) dissolve *17.2* – (sich) auflösen
door lock *16.3* – Türschloss
drill bit *9.2* – Bohrer
drill operator *20.1* – Bohrer/in
drilling *12.1* – Bohrloch
drive shaft *6.4* – Antriebs-, Getriebewelle
(to) drop forge *8.4* – gesenkschmieden
drop forging *8.3* – das Gesenkschmieden
ductile *4.1* – (ver)formbar, ausziehbar
ductility *4.2* – Verformbarkeit
durability *4.1* – Dauerhaftigkeit

E

earmuffs *19.2* – Ohrenschützer
ecologically safer *13.2* – ökologisch sicherer
(to) eject *11.2* – auswerfen
ejector *11.2* – Auswerfer
ejector pin *11.2* – Auswurfstift
elasticity *4.1* – Elastizität, Biegsamkeit
electrical connection *14.3* – Elektroanschluss
electrolyte *17.2* – Elektrolyt
electrostatic powder coating *18.2* – elektrostatische Pulverbeschichtung
elevator (AE), (BE: lift) *19.4* – Fahrstuhl, Aufzug
(to) eliminate *13.3* – beseitigen, abschaffen
(to) emerge *14.4* – austreten, hervortreten, erscheinen
emergency *19.1* – Notfall
emerging *10.4* – herauskommend
emery cloth *14.4* – Schmirgelleinen
emission *2.4* – Emission, Ausstoß, Abgase
employer *20.2* – Arbeitgeber/in
enclosure *20.3* – Anlage
energy source *7.4* – Energiequelle
engine piston *18.2* – Motorkolben
engineering *1.1* – Technik, Maschinenbau
enquiry *4.3* – Untersuchung
environment *18.1* – Umwelt, Umgebung
equation *15.1* – Gleichung
equivalent *10.2* – Entsprechung, Übersetzung
(to) estimate *17.1* – schätzen
(to) evacuate *19.4* – evakuieren, entleeren; räumen
excess *14.1* – überschüssig
excess heat *16.1* – Überschusshitze
(to) exert a force *13.1* – eine Kraft ausüben
exhaust gas *1.4* – Abgas

(to) expand 10.2 – sich ausdehnen, expandieren
expansion coefficient 13.3 – Ausdehnungskoeffizient
experience 20.2 – (Berufs-)Erfahrung
experiment 10.2 – Versuch, Experiment
(to) expose 13.3 – aussetzen
exposed 16.1 – ungeschützt
extinguished 19.4 – gelöscht
extruding 10.1 – das (Strang-)Pressen
extrusion process 10.4 – Extrusionsprozess, Strangpressprozess

F

factor 18.2 – Faktor
feature 6.4 – Eigenschaft
feed lever 7.3 – Vorschubhebel
fencing 18.3 – Einzäunung
fibreglass 13.3 – Glaswolle, -faser
(to) fill an order 20.2 – eine Bestellung ausführen
finishing 11.5 – Fertigstellung, Veredelung
fire breaks 19.4 – Feuer bricht aus
fire extinguisher 19.4 – Feuerlöscher
fire service 19.4 – Feuerwehr
fittings 1.1 – Armaturen
fixative 13.1 – Fixativ, Fixiermittel
flat file 5.3 – Flachfeile
flexible 13.3 – flexibel
flowchart 19.4 – Flussdiagramm
flush with 12.1 – eben, bündig (abschließend) mit
flux 14.4 – Fluss-, Schmelzmittel
forging 8.3 – das Schmieden
forklift (truck) 19.2 – Gabelstapler
foundry 11.3 – Gießerei
(to) fracture 4.1 – brechen, zerbrechen
frame 6.1 – Rahmen
free-standing 11.5 – frei stehend
friction 4.1 – Reibung
frictional force 15.1 – Reibungswiderstand, -kraft
frictional resistance 16.4 – Reibungswiderstand
funnel 11.2 – Trichter

G

galvanizing 8.1 – Galvanisierung
gap 12.5 – Lücke
gas offtake hood 2.3 – Gasabzugshaube
gear train 6.3 – Getriebe(räder)
gearbox 16.3 – Getriebe
(to) generate 15.3 – erzeugen
glassy matric epoxy 13.1 – glasartiges Matrix-Epoxidharz
glider 15.4 – Segelflugzeug
glue 13.2 – Klebstoff, Leim
glueing 8.1 – das Kleben
gold 1.3 – Gold
graphite 16.2 – Graphit
gravity 15.1 – Schwerkraft
(to) grind 11.5 – schleifen
grinder 6.1 – Schleifmaschine, Winkelschleifer
grinding 8.1 – das Schleifen
groove 9.3 – Nut
gutter 14.3 – Dachrinne

H

hacksaw 5.3 – Bügelsäge
half-round file 5.3 – Halbrundfeile
hand drill 5.1 – Handbohrer
handle 6.3 – (Hand-)Griff
hard hat 19.2 – Schutzhelm
hardness 4.1 – Härte, Festigkeit
hazardous 19.2 – gefährlich
head tube 14.1 – Hauptrohr
health 11.5 – Gesundheit
heat loss 2.4 – Wärmeverlust
heating duct 18.3 – Heizleitung
height gauge 3.1 – Höhenmesser

high-carbon steel 11.4 – Hartstahl, kohlenstoffreicher Stahl
highlighted 10.2 – hervorgehoben
high-powered 13.3 – Hochleistungs-
high tensile 13.3 – stark dehn- oder streckbar
hinge 16.4, 7.2 – Scharnier
hose 14.1 – Schlauch
hot dip galvanizing 18.3 – Feuerverzinkung
hub 15.3 – (Rad-)Nabe
hub cap 18.1 – Radkappe
Human Resources 20.2 – Personalabteilung
hydraulic ram 8.3 – hydraulische Ramme
hydrochloric acid 18.4 – Salzsäure
hydrogen 17.2 – Wasserstoff

I

(to) ignite 14.1 – anzünden
impurity 1.4 – Verunreinigung , Beimengung
in due course 20.3 – zu gegebener Zeit
incident 19.4 – Vorfall, Zwischenfall
increase 15.3 – Erhöhung
instruction 10.2 – Anweisung, Anleitung
instructor 11.3 – Ausbilder/in
internal combustion engine 12.1 – Verbrennungsmotor
iron 1.1 – Eisen
iron oxide 17.2 – Eisenoxyd

J

jaws 3.2 – Backen
joining 8.1 – das Fügen
jug 17.3 – Krug, Becher

K

kinetic friction 15.1 – kinetische Reibung
knife (pl. knives) 11.5 – Messer

L

laser cutter 9.3 – Laserschneidgerät
lathe 9.3 – Drehmaschine
lathe operator 20.1 – Dreher/in
layer 18.2 – Schicht
lead 1.2 – Blei
leather 13.3 – Leder
lethal 19.2 – tödlich
light unit 18.1 – Leuchteinheit
limestone 1.4 – Kalkstein
locating screw 13.1 – Halteschraube
location 13.1 – Ort, Platz
lock nut 12.1 – Überwurf-, Gegenmutter
locking clamp 7.3 – Feststellschraube
locking device 12.1 – Haltevorrichtung
locking wire 12.1 – Sperrdraht
low-carbon steel 11.4 – Flussstahl, kohlenstoffarmer Stahl
lubricant 15.1 – Gleit-, Schmiermittel
lubrication 15.0 – Schmierung

M

machine tool 16.3 – Werkzeugmaschine
machining 9.3 – maschinell bearbeiten
magnesium 2.1 – Magnesium
(to) maintain 16.1 – beibehalten; aufrechterhalten, bewahren
maintenance 12.1 – Wartung
malleable 2.1 – (ver)formbar
management 19.4 – Geschäftsleitung
manual 6.1 – Hand(arbeit); Benutzerhandbuch
manufacturer 11.5 – Fabrikant/in
manufacturing plant 19.4 – Produktionsstätte, Werk
manufacturing process 2.4 – Produktionsprozess
marble 11.5 – Marmor
masonry 6.2 – Mauerwerk, Beton
mass production 18.3 – Massenproduktion
master cylinder 15.3 – Bremszylinder
(to) melt 11.5 – schmelzen
melting point 11.4 – Schmelzpunkt
mercury 1.3 – Quecksilber
metal bucket 18.3 – Metalleimer

metal press 7.1 – Metallpresse
metal roofing 18.3 – Blechbedachung
metal shearing machine 7.1 – Schermaschine
metallurgist 11.5 – Metallurg/in
milling 8.1 – fräsen
milling machine 7.1 – Fräsmaschine
mix 14.1 – Mischung
mobility 7.4 – Beweglichkeit, Mobilität
moist 17.1 – feucht, nass
mold (BE, AE: mould) 1.4 – Form
molten iron 1.4 – geschmolzenes Eisen
motor shaft 6.4 – Motorwelle
moulded plastic 18.1 – Spritzkunststoff
(to) multiply (by) 15.2 – multiplizieren (mit)
multi-purpose 13.3 – Mehrzweck-
muscle power 7.4 – Muskelkraft

N

noble metals 1.1 – Edelmetalle
non-corrosive 13.3 – rostfrei
non-flammable 16.1 – nicht entzündbar
non-porous 13.3 – nicht porös
nozzle 9.4 – Düse
nut 5.2 – Mutter

O

oil sump 16.5 – Ölwanne
oil-based 13.3 – auf Ölbasis
on site 11.5 – auf der Baustelle, vor Ort
opaque 1.1 – undurchsichtig
open day 18.4 – Tag der offenen Tür
open-end spanner 5.1 – Gabel-, Schraubenschlüssel
operator 7.4 – Maschinist/in
ore 1.4 – Erz
outlet 1.4 – Auslass
(to) overcome 15.3 – überwinden
oxygen 14.1 – Sauerstoff
oxygen lance 2.4 – Sauerstofflanze

P

packing 18.4 – Verpackung
painting 8.1 – das Lackieren
parallax 3.1 – Parallaxe
pedestrian 19.1 – Fußgänger/in
permanent-mould casting 11.1 – Guss mit permanenten Formen
phosphorus 2.1 – Phosphor
pickling 18.4 – das (Ab-)Beizen
pig iron 1.4 – Roheisen
pipe 1.3 – Rohr, Röhre
piston 3.4 – Kolben
planetary gears 6.4 – Planetengetriebe
plant security 19.4 – Werkschutz
plasticene 11.5 – Plastilin, Knetmasse
plate 8.3 – Platte, Teller
platform 13.1 – Bodenplatte
platinum 4.1 – Platin
pliers 5.1 – (Kombi-)Zange
plunger 11.2 – Stampfer
(to) polish 6.1 – polieren
polishing 11.5 – das Polieren
polyurethane epoxy 13.1 – Polyurethan-Epoxidharz
porous 13.3 – porös
portable 7.4 – transportabel, tragbar
positioning 3.3 – Position(ierung)
pouring cup 11.1 – Gießtrichter
powder coating 10.3 – Pulverbeschichtung
power buffer 6.1 – Elektropolierer
power drill 6.1 – Elektrobohrer
power hacksaw 6.1 – elektrischer Fuchsschwanz
power screwdriver 6.1 – Akkuschrauber
power wrench 6.1 – elektrischer Schraubenschlüssel
precise 9.3 – genau, präzise
preheated 1.4 – vorgewärmt
(to) press 8.3 – pressen, drücken
pressing 8.1 – das Pressen

pressure 10.4 – Druck
pressure casting 11.1 – Spritzguss
pressure regulator 14.1 – Druckregler
pressure-resistant 16.1 – druckbeständig
pressurised 9.4 – Druck-
printed circuit 14.3 – gedruckter Schaltkreis
procedure 19.4 – Vorkehrung, Maßnahme
processing 1.4 – Be-, Verarbeitung
production engineering 9.3 – Fertigungs-technik
profile 10.3 – Profil
property 1.1 – Eigenschaft
protective gloves 19.2 – Schutz-, Arbeits-handschuhe
pulley safety guard 7.3 – Riementrieb-abdeckung
punching 8.1 – das Stanzen
punching machine 7.1 – Stanzmaschine
punctuation 13.4 – Zeichensetzung

Q

qualifications 20.2 – Qualifikationen, Zeugnisse
quality control 18.4 – Qualitätskontrolle
quenching 18.4 – das Abschrecken, Abkühlen
quill drive 7.3 – Spindelantrieb

R

radiator 18.1 – Heizkörper, Kühler
radiator grill 18.1 – Kühlergitter
railway line 17.1 – (Bahn-)Gleis
ratchet 5.2 – Ratsche
rates of pay 20.2 – Gehaltsstufen
ratio 14.1 – Verhältnis
(to) reduce 6.4 – reduzieren, verringern
reduction ratio 6.4 – Untersetzungs-verhältnis
reference 20.2 – Referenz, (Arbeits-)Zeugnis
refractory lining 1.4 – feuerfeste Auskleidung, Schamottverkleidung
reliability 12.1 – Zuverlässigkeit
removable 12.1 – abnehmbar
repair 12.1 – Reparatur
repair kit 13.3 – Reparatursatz, -werkzeuge
reshaping 8.1 – das Umformen
resistance 13.1 – Widerstand, Belastung
resistant 4.1 – beständig, widerstandsfähig
result 3.4 – Resultat, Ergebnis
retractable 3.2 – versenkbar, verschiebbar
review 7.4 – Zusammenfassung, Wieder-holung
ring gear 6.4 – Ringgetriebe
ring spanner 5.1 – Ringschlüssel
rivet 12.1 – Niete
rod 9.1 – Stange
rolling 10.1 – das Walzen
roof flashing 14.3 – Dachschutzblech
(to) rotate 3.4 – rotieren lassen; drehen
rotocasting 11.1 – Rotationsguss
rotor 15.3 – Rotor
rough sketch 19.3 – flüchtige Skizze
round file 5.3 – Rundfeile
rowing boat 15.4 – Ruderboot
rubber 18.1 – Gummi
rubber cement 13.3 – Gummilösung, Kautschukkitt
runner 11.1 – Laufrinne
rust 17.2 – Rost
rusting 17.1 – das Rosten

S

safety 19.1 – Sicherheit
safety sign 19.1 – Sicherheitsschild, -zeichen
sawblade 4.1 – Sägeblatt
scaffolder 20.1 – Gerüstbauer
scale 3.1 – Skala, Maßstab
screw clamp 3.2 – Feststellschraube
sculptor 11.5 – Bildhauer/in
sealant 13.1 – Dichtungsmittel
seam 14.3 – Naht
section 11.5 – Teil

(to) secure 12.5 – sichern, sicherstellen
self-tapping screw 12.1 – Bohrschraube, gewindebohrende Schraube
self-levelling 13.3 – selbst ausgleichend
separate 13.4 – getrennt
shaping 10.1 – Verformungsprozesse
shearing 8.2 – das Scheren
shearing machine 9.3 – Schermaschine
sheet metal cutters 5.3 – Blechschneider
sheetmetal worker 20.1 – Blecharbeiter/in
sheet steel 2.1 – Stahlblech
shelf (pl. shelves) 16.3 – Regal, Ablage
shipbuilding 11.5 – Schiff(s)bau
side-effects 16.1 – Nebenwirkungen
silica 2.1 – Kieselerde, Quarz
(door) sill 18.1 – Türschwelle
silver 1.3 – Silber
site (building site) 20.2 – Baustelle
slag 1.4 – Schlacke
slagging hole 2.4 – Schlackenloch
(to) smooth 5.3 – glätten
snowmobile 16.3 – Motorschlitten
socket bolt 12.1 – Kopfschraube
socket spanner 5.1 – Steckschlüssel
sodium 1.2 – Natrium
(to) solder 14.3 – löten
soldering 14.0 – das Löten
(to) solidify 11.2 – härten, fest werden; erstarren, verdichten
solution 13.3 – Lösung
solvent 13.3 – Lösungsmittel
sound insulation padding 13.1 – Schall-dämmung
span 4.3 – (Brücken-)Bogen
specification 9.5 – Angabe
(to) specify 10.4 – angeben, bestimmen, präzisieren
speed 9.5 – Geschwindigkeit
spin 6.4 – Drehung
(to) split 13.4 – (auf)teilen, spalten
split pin 12.1 – Splint
spray 17.2 – Sprühnebel
spring 4.2 – Feder
spring washer 12.1 – Federring, -scheibe
sprue 11.1 – Gießloch, Einguss
stainless steel 4.1 – rostfreier Stahl
starter (motor) 13.1 – Anlasser
static friction 15.1 – Haftreibung, ruhende Reibung
stationary 8.4 – (fest)stehend
statue 11.5 – Statue, Standbild
steel bar 3.1 – Stahlstab
steel mill 1.4 – Stahlwerk
steel shell 2.4 – Stahlmantel
steelmaker 20.1 – Stahlkocher
stem 3.2 – Tiefenmessstange
stone 11.5 – Stein
straight-cut head 5.2 – Einfachschlitzkopf
(to) straighten 10.4 – gerade machen, ausrichten
strength 13.3 – Kraft, Stärke
(to) stretch 8.3 – strecken, dehnen, spannen
structure 4.3 – Bau
stud 12.1 – Zapfen, Stift
(to) submit 20.2 – einreichen
substrate 13.3 – Untergrund
sulphur 2.1 – Schwefel
sun gear 6.4 – Sonnengetriebe
(to) supervise 7.4 – beaufsichtigen, kontrollieren
support 4.3 – Stütze
surface 3.3, 18.2 – (Ober-)Fläche
surplus 8.4 – überschüssig
(to) sway 4.3 – schwingen, schwanken
swing-door 19.1 – Schwingtür
switch 7.3 – Schalter

T

tab washer 12.1 – Sicherungsblech mit Nase
table 11.4 – Tabelle; 7.3– Tisch
tap 18.2 – (Wasser-)Hahn

tape 13.2 – Klebeband
taphole 1.4 – (Ab-)Stichloch
(to) temper 16.4 – härten, rasch abkühlen
temperature range 16.1 – Temperatur-bereich
tempering 8.1 – das Härten
textiles 13.3 – Textilien
thickness 3.2 – Dicke
threaded hole 12.1 – Gewindeloch
tight 9.3 – eng, knapp
tile 13.3 – Kachel, Fliese
tin 1.3 – Zinn
tip 14.1 – Spitze
tolerances 9.3 – Toleranzen
tongs 5.3 – (Schmiede-)Zange
tool container 10.4 – Werkzeugbehälter
tooth washer 12.1 – Zahnscheibe
torque (twist) 6.1 – Drehmoment, -kraft
toxic 2.4 – giftig, toxisch
toxic substance 19.2 – Giftstoff
traffic lights 17.1 – (Verkehrs-)Ampel
trainee 11.3 – Auszubildende/r
(to) transmit 15.3 – übertragen
trial and error 15.1 – Versuch und Irrtum, Ausprobieren
tubing 2.1 – Röhren
tungsten steel 4.1 – Wolframstahl
tuyere 1.4 – Winddüse, Lufteinlass
tyre 9.5 – Reifen

V

valve cover 13.1 – Ventilhaube
variable 4.3 – veränderlich, unterschiedlich
vernier callipers (AE: calipers) 3.1 – Mess-schieber
versatile 13.3 – vielseitig
versatility 13.3 – Vielseitigkeit
vinyl 13.3 – Vinyl
viscosity 11.5 – Viskosität, Konsistenz
voltage 19.2 – Spannung
volume 15.3 – Volumen

W

walkway 19.1 – Laufweg
washer 9.2 – Unterleg-, Dichtungsscheibe
waste product 1.4 – Abfallprodukt
water-absorbant 16.4 – Wasser aufnehmend
water-based 13.3 – auf Wasserbasis
water-cooled 2.3 – wassergekühlt
watering can 1.3 – Gießkanne
waterjet cutter 9.3 – Wasserstrahlschneid-anlage
watertightness 14.3 – Wasserundurch-lässigkeit
weakness 11.5 – Weichheit
wear 3.3 – Verschleiß, Abnutzung
weighing 18.4 – das Wiegen
weight 11.5 – Gewicht
welded joint 12.1 – Schweißverbindung
welding 8.1 – das Schweißen
welding torch 6.1 – Schweißbrenner
wheel rim 4.2 – Felge
wheelbarrow 18.2 – Schubkarre
windscreen 18.1 – Windschutzscheibe
windscreen wipers 18.1 – Scheibenwischer
wire 2.1 – Draht
wire cutters 5.3 – Seitenschneider, Drahtzange
(to) withstand 4.1 – aushalten
wood 13.3 – Holz
workpiece 3.1 – Werkstück
workplace 19.1 – Arbeitsplatz
wrench 4.2 – Schraubenschlüssel

Z

zinc 1.1 – Zink
zinc carbonate 18.3 – Zinkcarbonat
zinc oxide 18.3 – Zinkoxid